Patchwork Palette

NO-FAIL COLOR PLANS FOR CAPTIVATING QUILTS

Donna Lynn Thomas

Martingale
Create with Confidence

Dedication

To my adorable and adored granddaughter, Charlotte, who may one day grow to love quilts and quiltmaking as much as her mother, Katie, and I do. You are the light of my life, Sunshine!

Patchwork Palette:
No-Fail Color Plans for Captivating Quilts
© 2013 by Donna Lynn Thomas

Martingale®
19021 120th Ave. NE, Ste. 102
Bothell, WA 98011-9511 USA
ShopMartingale.com

Mission Statement

Dedicated to providing quality products and service to inspire creativity.

Printed in China
18 17 16 15 14 13   8 7 6 5 4 3 2 1

Library of Congress Cataloging-in-Publication Data is available upon request.

ISBN: 978-1-60468-143-7

CREDITS

President & CEO: Tom Wierzbicki

Editor in Chief: Mary V. Green

Design Director: Paula Schlosser

Managing Editor: Karen Costello Soltys

Acquisitions Editor: Karen M. Burns

Technical Editor: Laurie Baker

Copy Editor: Melissa Bryan

Production Manager: Regina Girard

Illustrator: Christine Erikson

Cover & Text Designer: Adrienne Smitke

Photographer: Brent Kane

Contents

Bonus Project Online: Mountain High
    Visit ShopMartingale.com/extras for complete instructions.

Introduction

I am an unapologetic fabric collector! I've been collecting fabric since the late '70s, and I love to use lots and lots of prints in my quilts. In my mind, the more prints the merrier!

Quilters generally have two ways of choosing an array of fabrics for a quilt. The first, a fixed palette, is a very traditional method relied on by most quilters: choose two to six prints and use them in the same fashion in each block and throughout the entire quilt.

"Blades," a fixed-palette quilt, from Flip Your Way to Fabulous Quilts *(Martingale, 2011); machine pieced by Donna Lynn Thomas and machine quilted by Sandy Gore*

The second approach is to use a variety of fabrics—a scrappy palette. Many times we choose and use fabrics in scrap quilts based on value (i.e., dark, medium, and light) without regard to color. Prints are sorted into three piles—darks, mediums, and lights—and then mixed randomly in each block and subsequently within the quilt as a whole. Usually each piece in a block is cut from a different print.

"Truly Nancy," a traditional scrap quilt, hand pieced and hand quilted by Nancy Wakefield

Although I love nothing better than using lots of prints in my quilts, I find the task of sorting all those prints, with no control over where each color goes, quite daunting. And many blocks simply don't lend themselves to a traditional value-based scrap approach.

As a result, I've come up with a unique way of blending the concepts of fixed and scrappy palettes. My quilts are not scrap quilts in the true sense of the word, but rather what I call multi-fabric recipe quilts. In "The Fabric Recipes," beginning on page 9, I'll introduce you to Rainbow, Color Family, and Mixed recipes in detail along with some basic concepts on how to create good fabric palettes based on the principles of hue, value, and variety of print scale.

With these recipes, you'll be able to create finished quilts that use lots of prints, are dynamic, and are full of color that is placed where you want it to be.

My fabric-recipe approach offers several advantages.

- You don't have to work with a large number of fabrics at a time—just a comfortably small fixed palette for each block or each set of blocks.

- You don't need large quantities of any particular fabric and you still get to use a lot of fabrics in your quilt. It's a great way to use all those manufacturer's precut fabrics we collect.

- You don't have to cut an entire quilt at one time—just the block set you're working on.

- You can build your quilt one set of blocks at a time over a span of time as you collect or put together new sets of prints. Your pile of block sets can grow quietly in a corner until you're ready to assemble the quilt top.

- You won't become bored, because the fabrics change with each new set of blocks and it's like working on a whole new quilt.

- It's a fun, easygoing way to make a quilt, and the concept is especially good for group quilts.

Put the recipe-based concept into practice with the 13 quilt patterns I've provided for inspiration. For added versatility, each project includes an alternate version using a different recipe and theme. You'll find guidelines on how to increase or decrease the size of your quilt either by making more or fewer block sets or, alternatively, making more or fewer blocks in each set. Don't let the size of my quilts deter you from making whatever quilt size you want. I don't want you to be limited to what you see here—use my ideas as a jumping-off point for your own.

Now on to the *Patchwork Palette*!

Quiltmaking Techniques

The techniques covered here are ones that I refer to often throughout the projects in this book. While you may have other ways of accomplishing the same tasks, these are my favorite methods because they consistently result in precise, accurate pieces. For basic quiltmaking instructions, such as for rotary cutting, adding borders, and completing your quilt, go to www.ShopMartingale.com/HowtoQuilt.

ADD-AN-INCH BIAS SQUARES

Bias squares (also known as half-square-triangle units or triangle squares) are traditionally composed of two half-square triangles sewn together along their long bias edges. Normally, to make bias squares, we cut half-square triangles from squares that are ⅞" larger than the desired finished size of the short edge of the triangle. Unfortunately, once the triangles are sewn together, the resulting bias squares are often distorted or inaccurate in size.

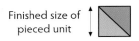
Finished size of pieced unit

With add-an-inch bias squares, you cut and sew slightly oversized triangles to make slightly oversized bias squares, and then trim the bias squares to the required size. The result is perfectly sized bias squares every time with a minimum of effort. I like to use the Bias Square® ruler for trimming the bias squares to size, but any square ruler with a 45°-angle line will do the trick.

To begin, cut half-square triangles from squares that are 1" larger than the finished size, instead of the more precise ⅞" (hence the name "add-an-inch bias squares"). For example, here are the steps for making two bias squares that will finish to 2".

1. Choose two prints for the bias squares and from each print cut a 3" square (1" larger than the desired 2" finished size).

2. Place the two squares right sides together.

3. Cut the pair of squares in half diagonally to make two pairs of half-square triangles.

4. Sew each pair of triangles on their bias edges using ¼" seam allowances. Press carefully, keeping the iron on the straight grain so as not to distort or stretch the seam.

5. Trim each bias square to 2½" (trim size = finished size + ½") using the Bias Square ruler. Place the diagonal line of the ruler on the seam of the bias square when you trim each of the four sides.

Place diagonal line of ruler on seam line. Trim first two sides.

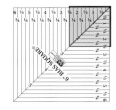
Align desired measurement on previously cut edge and diagonal line on seam. Trim remaining sides.

FOLDED CORNERS

The basic idea of folded corners is to sew a square of fabric to the corner of a larger "parent" square, and then fold over the smaller square to duplicate a corner triangle. Use the following simple step-by-step process to make folded-corner units.

1. Determine the finished size of the corner triangle where it falls on the side of the main unit. Add ½" to this measurement and cut a square this size. In the example given, you would cut a 2½" square to sew onto the 4" finished parent square.

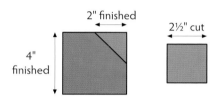

2. Draw a diagonal line on the wrong side of the smaller corner square. This line must be very fine and accurate, running exactly from corner to corner. To keep the fabric from shifting as you mark, place the square on a sandpaper board or super-fine sandpaper. To further reduce shifting, hold your pencil at a 45° angle so the point doesn't drag in the weave of the fabric. Carefully place the smaller square on the corner of the larger parent unit with right sides together. Sew just to the right of the marked line.

Draw line.   Stitch just to the right of the line.

No-Mark Method

Consider using the Angler 2 stitching template instead of drawing diagonal lines on each square. It's designed specifically with this purpose in mind. The packet includes clear, easy-to-follow instructions for setting up the guide on your sewing machine, and the Angler 2 also provides a guideline for sewing perfect ¼"-wide seam allowances.

3. Press the small square back over the corner, right side facing up, and check it for accuracy. Be careful not to stretch it. It should lie exactly on the corner of the parent unit. If it doesn't, check the accuracy of the marked line or your sewing and adjust as needed. If the square comes up short of the corner, you may need to sew a thread's width closer to the corner of the unit. If the square is too big for the corner, check to make sure you're sewing exactly from corner to corner and your pieces are lined up properly. If there's consistent trouble, check the accuracy of the

corner-square size, the parent-unit size, the drawn line, or your sewing to find and correct the source of the problem. Each seam must be accurate in order for your final unit to finish at the size it's meant to be.

Fold square over corner.

4. Trim away both extra layers of fabric under the top corner triangle, trimming ¼" from the stitching line.

Improve Your Accuracy

Here are some additional tips to help ensure your success with the folded-corners technique.

- Use an open-toe or clear presser foot so you can see to place the first corner precisely in front of the needle.

- Use a straight-stitch throat plate, if you have one, to keep corners from being sucked into the larger hole of a regular throat plate and mangled.

- Lift your presser foot slightly to place each piece under the foot. Running it under the lowered presser foot without lifting can misalign the top piece.

- Always sew with the corner to be trimmed away to the right of the needle. This is very important or you'll often end up with folded corners that are too small.

- Some machines lose control of the far corners as they sew. If this is a problem, pin through the layers in the right corner to keep them from shifting as you sew. Because the pin is positioned out of the way of the oncoming needle, you don't need to remove it to prevent needle breakage. You don't usually need a pin in the first corner because it goes directly under the presser foot.

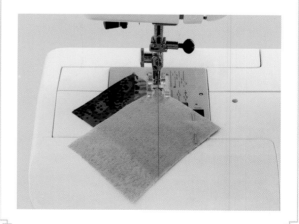

The Fabric Recipes

I love to use lots and lots of fabrics in quilts—but in a controlled manner. What's even more fun is to let each print shine in its very own block and not get lost in the crowd. To this end, I've devised an approach that adapts the concept of a fixed color palette to making multi-fabric quilts.

Instead of using lots of prints randomly in each block, I make one or more blocks at a time from a fixed palette of prints. Then, when I make the next set of blocks, I use a new fixed palette of prints. In this way I only have to work with a few prints at a time and I only need to cut and sew one set of blocks at a time if I wish.

Look at the two blocks below. One uses just two fabrics in addition to the background print, allowing all of the prints to be showcased in one block. The other is a totally scrappy block where each piece is cut from a different print. See the difference?

The same block using a fixed palette (left) and a scrappy palette (right)

I also tend to mix fixed and scrappy palettes when it comes to finishing the quilt beyond the blocks themselves. Sometimes I use just one print for side setting triangles or sashing pieces, and other times I make these pieces out of a mix of fabrics left over from the blocks. It all depends on what look I want and what I have in my stash or see in the store. Sometimes I piece borders using leftover prints from the quilt center, and sometimes I use a theme print that coordinates with all the other prints. Some quilts don't even need borders. The rules are pretty loose as to what I do once the blocks are together.

Let's look at the three color recipes I use when I make my quilts. They each provide varying degrees of control of the selection process, making it easy to work with a lot of prints in one quilt.

THE RAINBOW RECIPE

This recipe is the liveliest of the three. With this recipe, you choose the colors and prints for one set of blocks and then make them. When those blocks are finished, you choose the prints for the next set of blocks using a completely new set of colors and prints. The result is a rainbow of colors in your quilt.

Rainbow-recipe quilts are fun to make because each set of blocks lets you use all kinds of color and print combinations. You can use a wide range of color families or limit them to a handful. Changing the placement of the values along with the colors in each set of blocks is another way to add interest, but be aware that the overall effect will also change. The fun part about this recipe is that you can really play in your stash!

Let's look at the Double Pinwheel blocks shown. Each block is made from a completely different set of prints. Once the blocks are sewn together, the resulting quilt will be lively and colorful.

THE COLOR FAMILY RECIPE

Most quilters prefer a little more control in the use of color, which is why this recipe is probably the most comfortable. As with any fixed-palette quilt, you make color assignments for each position in the block. Then you choose a print for each color assignment. This becomes your Color Family recipe for all subsequent block sets that you make.

You can clearly see the Color Family recipe in the Double Pinwheel blocks shown below— large green pinwheels and small purple pinwheels all on a cream background print. To create a quilt using the Color Family recipe, make each new set of blocks with a fresh set of green, purple, and cream prints following the same color assignments.

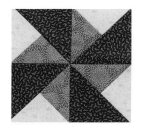

Mix It Up!

Be careful not to overmatch your color families. If you're using reds, choose cherry reds, brownish reds, purplish reds, and possibly a bit of orange to enliven the quilt and make it sparkle. If all the prints are the same exact color, you might as well stick with just one print.

THE MIXED RECIPE

This is probably the loosest recipe of all. You can mix up elements of Rainbow and Color Family recipes in one quilt, or even sprinkle in a bit of a fixed palette if you wish. In essence, you can do pretty much whatever you want. Here are some combinations to try.

- Choose one part of the block and use the same fabric for that portion of every block, just as you would in a traditional fixed-palette quilt. For the other pieces, use a Rainbow or Color Family recipe. Some of the Mixed-recipe quilts in the book use one background print for all the blocks.
- If your quilt is made up of two blocks that alternate throughout the quilt, make one from a Rainbow recipe and the other from a Color Family recipe.
- Make all the blocks from a Rainbow recipe but reserve one position, or more, in the block for a Color Family assignment.

Let's take another look at that Double Pinwheel block. In this example, the large pinwheel color changes with each set of blocks, but the small pinwheel color and the background color remain the same in every set. You could do the reverse, making the large pinwheels from the same color in each block set and changing the color of the small pinwheels. It's all up to you.

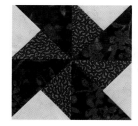

Selecting Fabrics

With any quilt, whether you're using a "recipe" or not, combining the right fabrics is key to a successful project. Some quilters think the hardest part about making a quilt is picking the fabrics, while some like this part of the process the best. Often the difference between enjoying the process and fearing it is simply a matter of understanding some basic principles of fabric selection.

There are three basic concepts that guide me when selecting fabrics for any quilt, whether it will have a fixed palette or a multi-fabric palette. Keep in mind that the recipe quilts in this book consist of sets of blocks each made from fixed-palette combinations, so the same three principles apply.

When you make a quilt block, you cut fabric into smaller pieces and sew them back together to create a design. You wouldn't cut up one piece of fabric into all the pieces for a block and sew them back together, because you wouldn't be able to see the design. You need contrast between the pieces in order to create the block design. Therefore, you need to use different pieces of fabric for different parts of the block. The three tools we use to create *contrast* are hue (color), value (dark and light), and, to a lesser extent, variety of scale in the prints selected. To make good fabric choices for a block or quilt, let's explore each of these three topics in a little more detail.

HUE

Hue is color. It's the primary aspect we notice when we look at a quilt, unless it's a black-and-white or other color-neutral quilt. A discussion of color is difficult without a basic color wheel, so I've provided a useful color-wheel quilt for reference (above right).

Primary, Secondary, and Tertiary Colors

The largest spokes on the color-wheel quilt represent the *primary* colors—red, blue, and yellow. They are equidistant from each other on the wheel as well. All other colors are derived from these three primary colors.

When you mix two primary colors you create *secondary* colors, which are represented by the medium-sized spokes on the color-wheel quilt. They're also equidistant from each other, falling between the primary colors.

When you mix a primary color and a secondary color you create a *tertiary* color. These colors fall between their primary and secondary parents and are represented by the smallest spokes on the wheel.

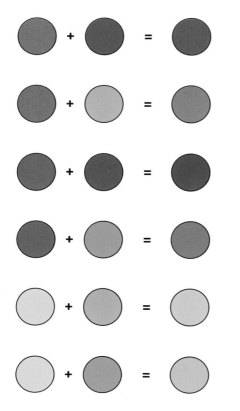

Brown is the mix of equal parts of the three primary colors. It's the perfect neutral. All colors combine well with pure brown.

Black is the absence of all color and white is the presence of all color.

Shades, Tints, and Tones

Most of us don't work with pure hues very often. We generally use what are called shades, tints, and tones of color.

Shades of a color are a pure color with black added to it. Depending on how much black you add, the shade becomes just a little darker or a lot darker than the original pure color.

Tints of a color have white added to a pure hue. Again, depending on how much white is added, the tint can range from slightly paler than the original hue all the way down to just a hint of color.

Pure gray is half black and half white. When gray is added to a pure hue, it creates a *tone* of that color. When a color has been toned down, that means the color has a grayish quality to it.

Combining Colors

So what do we do with this information? Well, there are five basic combinations we derive from the color wheel that will provide good results every time. I'll cover four of the combinations here, leaving *monochromatic* for later when we discuss value. No matter whether you're working with tints, tones, or shades of a color, the principles given here for combining colors will apply.

The first and simplest combination is called a *complementary* combination. This is a combination of any two colors directly opposite each other on the color wheel. If you want just two colors in a quilt, select the first color and look for its complement on the color wheel. Red and green are an example of a complementary combination on the color wheel. We've seen this combination used successfully throughout quilt history.

The second combination is called *triadic*. This involves three colors equidistant from each other on the color wheel. Red, blue, and yellow—the primary colors—are a triad. There are many others as well. See what other triads you can find on the color-wheel quilt.

A third way to combine colors is by using the colors on either side of the main color. This is called an *analogous* combination. Using blue as a main color, and teaming it with blue-purple and blue-green, is a good example of such a combination.

Another easy approach is to use the *split complement* of a color. As discussed above, complementary colors are directly opposite each other. A split-complementary combination is made up of the two colors on each side of the complement of the main color. For example, the complement of purple (the main color) is yellow. The split complement would be the colors on either side of yellow: yellow-orange and yellow-green. If you need more than three colors, you can take two or more colors on either side of the complement instead of just one on either side.

There are many other ways of using the color wheel to help you select fabric. Consider buying a good pocket color wheel. It will contain all the above information as well as instructions on how to "dial up" many other successful color combinations.

Warm and Cool Colors

One other very important aspect of color is the concept of warm and cool colors. Warm colors are the colors of fire, such as red, orange, and yellow. Cool colors are the colors of water and trees, such as blue, green, and purple. Warm colors are very aggressive. They appear to jump out from the surface of a quilt yelling, "Look at me!" Cool colors recede, trying not to draw attention to themselves. Therefore, it's very important to balance your warm and cool colors in a quilt, depending on the effect you're trying to create. If you have a mostly cool quilt and add one touch of fiery red to part of the block, such as a pinwheel center, that red will become the focal point. All eyes will go there first before looking at the rest of the quilt. It can make quite an impact, which may or may not be what you want.

The warm red triangles in this Pinwheel block come forward, while the cool blue triangles recede.

If you're mixing warm and cool blocks in a quilt, be sure to balance them evenly throughout the quilt top, avoiding a cluster of warm or cool blocks in one section (unless that's the effect you're going for). Look at "Pipe Dreams" on page 20. I spent a good bit of time making sure the warm and cool blocks were placed evenly around the quilt top, ensuring that the eye moves evenly across the surface.

Beyond Color Theory

The four color combinations covered earlier—complementary, triadic, analogous, and split complementary—are a jumping-off point for fabric selection. Don't get too lost in the weeds of color theory. Quilters throughout history have used many other tried-and-true ways of combining color for their quilts.

One of the most popular ways is to find a gorgeous multicolored print you love, and then use colors from this print for your quilt. You don't even have to include this print in your quilt; it's just your inspiration. Also, remember that most, but not all, modern fabrics have color dots on the selvage indicating the dyes used in that print. Use these dots as a source of color inspiration too.

Look at the use of color in scrapbooking papers, wallpaper books, paintings, nature, and anywhere you find beautiful colors appearing together. Incorporate what you see out in the world into your quilt color combinations.

VALUE

Value is a term often mixed up with the word *contrast.* Contrast indicates a difference between two things, while value indicates the degree of dark and light. Value is just one way to create contrast.

Monochromatic (one-color) quilts use value to create design. "Carrie's Box" on page 75 is an excellent example of a monochromatic quilt that totally depends on value to create its visual effect. The three-dimensional aspect of the Folded Box block relies on the use of dark, medium, and light values of the same color. If I had used all medium values in the block or placed the different values in different positions, the three-dimensional appearance would have been lost.

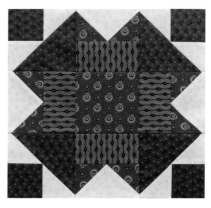

The careful use of value in the block on the top produces a three-dimensional effect, as if the sides of a box are folding in on itself. The block on the bottom was created with no consideration for value, resulting in a flat, two-dimensional aspect.

Value can also be used to create visual movement by grading elements from dark to light. Bargello and Trip Around the World quilts are excellent examples of this effect, as is the quilt shown below, "Shimmering Leaves" from *Flip Your Way to Fabulous Quilts*. The shimmer in the leaves comes from the gradation of dark to light in the striped rectangles.

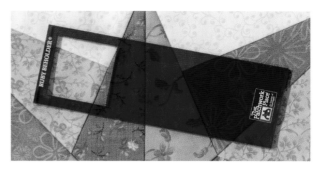

Use the Ruby Beholder to determine the value of your fabrics.

"Shimmering Leaves" from Flip Your Way to Fabulous Quilts; *machine pieced by Donna Lynn Thomas and machine quilted by Pam Goggans*

Use tools such as the Ruby Beholder® (above right) to help you determine value gradations without the visual interference of color on what you are seeing. If you look through the red filter, the effect of color is eliminated and you see just the value of the prints in front of you.

You can also use value to create unique design elements. Throughout the quilt "Walk in the Woods," shown below, are distinct, winding paths created by the dark and light triangles in each block. Color doesn't matter. Make this quilt from all kinds of color combinations and the paths still show, as long as the triangles in the block are dark and light. If the dark and light values were removed, the paths would disappear, taking the overall design with them.

"Walk in the Woods," machine pieced by Donna Lynn Thomas and machine quilted by Charlotte Freeman

Look at the two St. Louis Star blocks below. The beveled effect seen in the block on the left is created by the use of dark- and medium-value red prints and dark- and medium-value green prints. The block on the right uses colors of the same value and the bevel disappears.

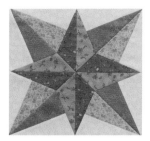 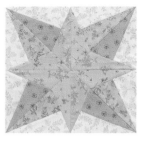

In the block on the left, a bevel effect is created where the dark and medium prints of the same color meet. The block on the right uses fabrics of the same value, which creates a flat effect.

Value is also useful for giving a quilt a certain feeling or mood. If you use mostly dark- and medium-value colors in your quilts, you create the popular primitive look. If you use mediums and lights, you create a soft pastel appearance. The next two blocks are examples of low value, meaning there isn't much value difference between the darkest and lightest prints. Look at the two different Pinwheel blocks: one shows low value with darks, and the other shows low value with lights.

 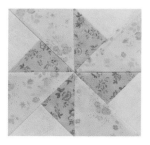

Low value results when fabrics with little difference in value are used together.

For high value, pair very dark and very light prints with each other. "With This Ring" on page 25 is an example of high-value contrast—dark fabrics used on a light background.

SCALE OF PRINT

Quilters collect and use all types of prints. We have so much available to us these days: stripes, checks, paisleys, batiks, big florals, little florals, ditsy prints, swirls, and all kinds of unique and fanciful patterns. Many quilters are timid and stick with all small-scale prints, afraid to venture into other types and sizes of motifs. Some quilters come from a garment-construction background where there are more stringent rules on what you can and can't combine to look good on a human body. Some are exuberant and use all the big prints they can find. So what do we do?

Visually interesting quilts bring together stripes, florals, paisleys, batiks, and all kinds of prints. But along with providing visual interest, it's also important to include places for the eye to rest. The balance of these two components is what matters.

If you use too much of the same small scale of print, your eye and brain will become bored. What started out as a pleasing and calm quilt can quickly slip into ho-hum. On the other side of the spectrum, too many large-scale prints can be chaotic, making a quilt almost painful to view for any length of time.

Look at the three blocks above right. The one on the top left is bland. The colors are nice, but an entire quilt of this block would become boring rather quickly. The block on the top right probably makes your teeth grind. With all the chaos of the large prints, you can barely see the distinction between the pieces in the blocks. The block on the bottom is more visually interesting. It uses a mix of print styles while still providing a place for the eye to rest.

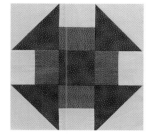

Mixing print types can mean the difference between bland (top left), chaotic (top right), and just right (bottom).

Used with care, different prints can produce all kinds of texture as well as visual movement. Prints can be fussy cut to create specific effects in both appliqué and piecing. Different prints can produce architectural effects in houses and subtle effects in flowers and portraits. With thoughtful placement, we can create altogether different effects from the original block design.

When choosing fabrics for a set of blocks, I always try to include a directional print, a larger floral or swirl of some type, and other distinct types of print. I rarely use a designer's collection in toto, because each collection contains a limited number of prints and colors and the quilt becomes overly matched for my taste. I love nothing better than to mix designers and use fabrics from years and decades past in a new quilt. No one else will have a quilt just like it.

Having said all this about prints, I must tell you that this book does contain one quilt I made from solids—my first one in more than 25 years. See "Gems" on page 49. These aren't ordinary solids, though—they're shot cottons from Michael Oakschott in England. The cottons are hand dyed and hand loomed in Kerala, India, and they have a soft iridescence reminiscent of silk. They're fascinating to gaze upon, don't look dimensionally flat, and practically demand to be touched. I'm not usually a fan of solids, but these are in a class by themselves. The lesson is to never be hard and fast in your rules and stay open to everything!

Practice makes perfect. The best way to become comfortable selecting fabrics for your quilts is to practice. You don't need big pieces of fabric to do this. Charm squares, manufacturer's precut pieces, and remnants work just fine. Without a particular quilt in mind, practice making beautiful arrays of prints on a table. When making your selections, keep in mind the principles of hue, value, and scale of print. Leave your palette, come back a day or so later, and see what you think. Play some more until you're pleased with the results. Take a picture so you'll remember what you've done, and then experiment some more with new prints and new ideas. The more you practice and play, the more comfortable you'll feel with the process.

The Quilts

In this section you'll find 13 fabric-recipe quilt patterns and photos of 26 quilts. Each quilt plan shows a photo of the main quilt for which the instructions are written, as well as a photo of the same quilt using an alternate fabric recipe. I don't want you to get stuck on just one look for a quilt!

All the quilts are made using sets of blocks in one of the three fabric recipes provided: Rainbow, Color Family, or Mixed. Keep in mind the principles of color, value, and scale of print when choosing the fabrics for each set of blocks.

Pressing instructions are carefully mapped out for you and are indicated by arrows in the assembly diagrams. Please follow them carefully so your seam allowances at intersections, especially block to block, will be pressed in opposite directions. Pay attention—some of the pressing directions are counterintuitive, but they'll make a difference as you complete your blocks and quilts. In a few instances, a perfect solution (all seams pressed in opposite directions) wasn't possible, so the best alternative has been provided.

Cutting and assembly instructions are given for making just one set of blocks, with separate instructions for completing the quilt top. Repeat the block-assembly instructions for all subsequent block sets, choosing and using new prints with each new set. I sort and cut my prints by block set in order to keep the pieces for each set together, not mixed up with other sets of prints.

CHANGING BLOCK SETS AND QUILT SIZES

Please note that some quilt settings require an odd total number of blocks, such as 13. This is the case in most on-point quilt settings and some horizontal settings that use two alternating blocks. If you're making seven pairs of blocks for a total of 14, but you need only 13, this will result in one leftover block—an orphan block. I don't mind this because I never know which block I'll want to eliminate until I have all the blocks on my design wall. If you prefer not to have a left-over block, I'll explain how to adjust the cutting instructions to make just one block for that final set, thus eliminating the orphan.

Because the blocks in my quilts are made in small sets, it's possible to increase or decrease the number of blocks you make in each block set. You may want to make a larger quilt and thus make more blocks within each set—for instance, three blocks per set instead of two as called for in the pattern. Or, you may want to end up with a smaller quilt and make fewer blocks in each set. In either case, it's a simple matter to figure out new cutting instructions.

Calculating the Cutting for a Single Block

Whether you plan to increase or decrease the number of blocks in a block set, it's important to first calculate the number of pieces to cut for a single block in a block set. To do this, divide the quantity of pieces indicated in the pattern for each print in the block by the number of blocks in the block set. This gives you the number of pieces you need for just one block. Use this to make the one extra block you need for an odd quilt set, or to make one block at a time instead of sets of blocks.

As a hypothetical example, let's say the cutting instructions call for four blocks in each set and you want to make just one block. The block cutting instructions would indicate:

From print 1, cut:
24 squares, 2½" x 2½"

From print 2, cut:
16 rectangles, 2½" x 4½"

From print 3, cut:
4 squares, 5" x 5"

To calculate the pieces of print 1 for one block, divide 24 squares by four (the number of blocks in the set) to get six. You now know to cut six squares for one block instead of 24. Divide the rest of the quantities in the cutting instructions for each print by four to calculate what you need for just one block.

> **Print 2:** 16 rectangles ÷ 4 = 4 rectangles
> **Print 3:** 4 squares ÷ 4 = 1 square

Changing the Number of Blocks in a Set

The easiest way to increase the size of a quilt is to make more block sets using even more prints. But you can also increase the number of blocks you make in each set. If you wish to increase or decrease the number of blocks in a block set, multiply each of the single-block quantities determined in the preceding example by the number of blocks you'd like to make. This tells you the number of pieces to cut for the new set of blocks.

Using the same example given above, let's say you want to make six blocks in each set instead of the four indicated in the cutting instructions. You would calculate the cutting for one block as we've already done. Then you would multiply by six to get the quantities needed for six blocks.

Cutting for one block (as calculated above)

> **Print 1:** 6 squares x 6 blocks = 36 squares
> **Print 2:** 4 rectangles x 6 blocks = 24 rectangles
> **Print 3:** 1 square x 6 blocks = 6 squares

SKILL LEVEL

The skill level for each quilt is indicated by rotary-cutter icons at the beginning of the project. One rotary cutter indicates the easiest quilts, two cutters signify a bit more of a challenge, and three cutters indicate more intricate piecing.

Easy

Intermediate

A Bit More Challenging

FABRIC DIMENSIONS

In the patterns I often refer to precut fabrics such as fat quarters and fat eighths. Here are the industry measurements for these pieces.

> Fat quarter = 18" x 22"
> Fat eighth = 9" x 22"

I've also used precut 5" and 10" squares in some of the quilts. These come in bundles and you'll simply need to take out the number of squares required for the project. If you don't have, use, or buy precut fabrics, you can use the dimensions above to ensure that the amount of fabric you do have will work.

I hope you enjoy these projects and go on to create more of your own recipe-quilt ideas!

Pipe Dreams

This beautiful and colorful Rainbow-recipe quilt has 18 blocks made one pair at a time from nine different dark-value bright, medium-value bright, and black prints. The setting triangles and pieced borders are all cut from the block leftovers plus three additional black prints.

FINISHED QUILT: 53" x 64¼" • FINISHED BLOCK: 8" x 8" • Make 18 blocks.

SKILL LEVEL:

MATERIALS

Yardage is based on 42"-wide fabric.

1 fat quarter *each* of 9 assorted black prints for blocks and inner and outer pieced borders

1 fat eighth *each* of 9 assorted dark-value bright prints and 9 assorted medium-value bright prints for blocks and middle pieced border

½ yard *each* of 3 assorted black prints for setting triangles and outer pieced border

½ yard of fabric for binding

3⅜ yards of fabric for backing (horizontal seam)

60" x 72" piece of batting

BLOCK CUTTING

Instructions are for cutting one pair of blocks. Before you begin cutting, make nine sets, with one dark-value bright print, one medium-value bright print, and one of the assorted black prints in each set. Repeat these instructions for each set to make nine pairs of blocks (18 blocks total) and the pieced borders. Cut the block sets separately in order to keep the prints in each set together.

From the dark-value bright print, cut:
1 strip, 1½" x 12"
1 strip, 1½" x 7"
4 rectangles, 1½" x 3½"
4 rectangles, 1½" x 2½"
1 strip, 2" x 11"

From the medium-value bright print, cut:
1 strip, 1½" x 12"
1 strip, 1½" x 7"
4 rectangles, 1½" x 3½"
4 rectangles, 1½" x 2½"
1 strip, 2" x 11"

From the black print, cut:
2 strips, 2½" x 12"
2 squares, 2½" x 2½"
4 strips, 1½" x 7"
8 rectangles, 1½" x 2½"
8 squares, 1½" x 1½"
1 strip, 2¼" x 19½"
1 strip, 6½" x 21"

CUTTING FOR THE REMAINING PIECES

From the 3 assorted black prints for setting triangles and outer pieced border, cut a *total* of:
3 squares, 14½" x 14½"; cut into quarters diagonally to make 12 side setting triangles
2 strips, 6½" x 21"

From the binding fabric, cut:
6 strips, 2¼" x 42"

Pieced by Donna Lynn Thomas; quilted by Freda Smith

BLOCK ASSEMBLY

Instructions are for making one pair of blocks at a time. Press all seam allowances in the direction of the arrows.

1. Select one set of block pieces. Join a black 1½" x 7" strip to each long edge of the dark 1½" x 7" strip to make strip unit A. Crosscut the strip unit into four segments, 1½" wide.

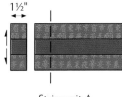

Strip unit A.
Make 1. Cut 4 segments.

2. Join a black 2½" x 12" strip to one long edge of the dark 1½" x 12" strip to make strip unit B. Crosscut the strip unit into four segments, 2½" wide.

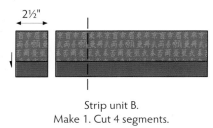

Strip unit B.
Make 1. Cut 4 segments.

3. Sew the remaining two black 1½" x 7" strips to the long edges of the medium 1½" x 7" strip to make strip unit C. Crosscut the strip unit into four segments, 1½" wide.

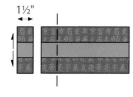

Strip unit C.
Make 1. Cut 4 segments.

4. Use the remaining black 2½" x 12" strip and the medium 1½" x 12" strip to make strip unit D. Crosscut the strip unit into four segments, 2½" wide.

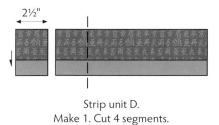

Strip unit D.
Make 1. Cut 4 segments.

5. Refer to "Folded Corners" on page 7 to sew a black 1½" square to one end of a medium 1½" x 3½" rectangle as shown. Repeat to make a total of four units.

Make 4.

6. Repeat step 5 using the dark 1½" x 3½" rectangles and the remaining black 1½" squares.

Make 4.

7. On the wrong side of a medium 1½" x 2½" rectangle, draw a diagonal line from the upper-left corner to 1½" down on the opposite side. With right sides together, place the marked rectangle on a black 1½" x 2½" rectangle as shown. Sew on the drawn line. Trim ¼" from the stitching line. Repeat to make a total of four units.

Make 4.

8. Repeat step 7 with the dark 1½" x 2½" rectangles and the remaining black 1½" x 2½" rectangles.

Make 4.

9. Using two each of the strip unit A and strip unit C segments and two of each unit from steps 5–8, assemble the two types of block corners as shown. Make four of each type.

Make 4.

Make 4.

10. Arrange two of each corner unit from step 9, one 2½" black square, and two each of the strip unit B and strip unit D segments into three horizontal rows as shown. Sew the units in each row together to make the block. Repeat to make a second block.

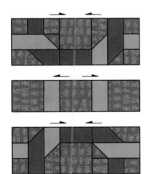 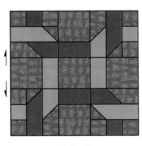

Make 2.

11. Repeat steps 1–10 with the remaining block sets to make a total of 18 blocks.

QUILT-TOP ASSEMBLY

1. Cut two black side setting triangles in half as shown to make four corner setting triangles.

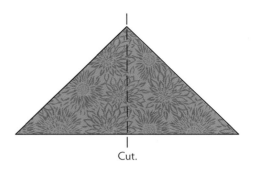

Cut.

2. Refer to the quilt assembly diagram on page 24 to lay out the blocks and side and corner setting triangles in diagonal rows. Balance the block colors and prints across the surface of the quilt and arrange the blocks so that the light bars on the edge of one block meet with the dark bars on the next block. Sew the blocks and side setting triangles in each diagonal row together. Join the rows. Add the corner setting triangles last. Trim the quilt top to ¼" from the block points.

3. Randomly sew the nine black 2¼" x 19½" strips together end to end to make one long strip. From this pieced strip, measure and cut two strips to fit the center length of the quilt top. Sew these strips to the sides of the quilt top. From the remainder of the pieced strip, measure and cut two strips to fit the center width of the quilt top. Sew these strips to the top and bottom of the quilt top.

4. Repeat step 3 with the dark and medium 2" x 11" strips to add the middle border to the quilt top. Use the assorted black 6½" x 21" strips to add the outer border to the quilt top in the same manner.

FINISHING

1. Layer the quilt top with batting and backing; baste the layers together.
2. Quilt as desired.
3. Bind the quilt edges with the 2¼"-wide binding strips.

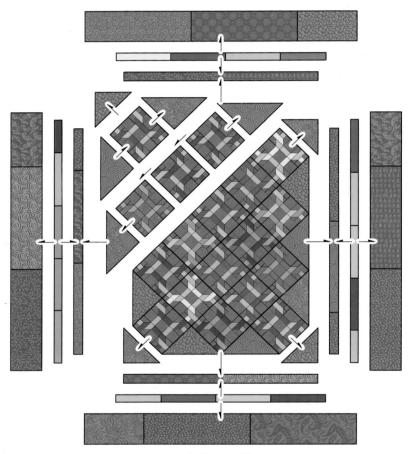

Quilt assembly

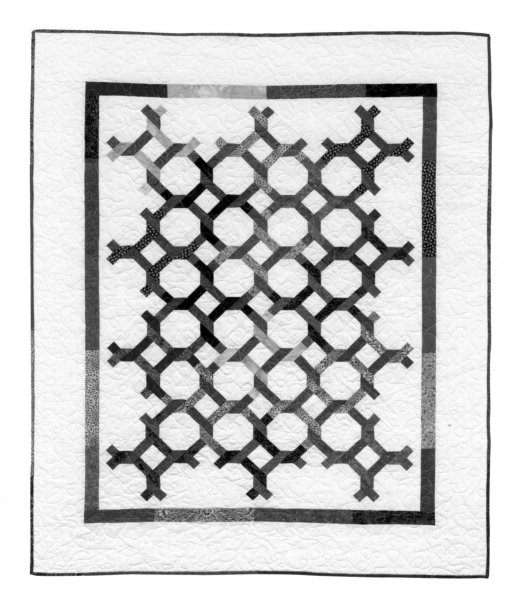

Color Option

"With This Ring," machine pieced and quilted by Kim Pope

Made as a wedding gift for Kim's son and daughter-in-law, this quilt shows off the Mixed recipe in patriotic colors, plus a single white print for the background and border. Notice the pieced binding using fabrics from the quilt blocks—what a nice way to bring the colors out to the edge.

Goose Chase

This rich Color Family–recipe quilt is based on the beautiful directional floral border print, which was cut along the lengthwise grain. Notice how the flowers "chase" each other around the border. Both the Goose in the Pond blocks and the Single Irish Chain blocks are made one pair at a time using a Color Family recipe. Choose four prints for the Goose in the Pond blocks and two prints for the Single Irish Chain blocks.

FINISHED QUILT: 78¾" x 78¾" • FINISHED BLOCK: 11¼" x 11¼"
Make 13 Goose in the Pond blocks and 12 Single Irish Chain blocks.

SKILL LEVEL:

MATERIALS

Yardage is based on 42"-wide fabric.

½ yard *each* of 6 assorted cream prints for Single Irish Chain blocks

2½ yards of multicolored print for outer border (cut lengthwise OR 1⅝ yards if cut crosswise)

1 fat quarter *each* of 7 assorted cream prints for Goose in the Pond blocks

1 fat quarter *each* of 7 assorted cinnamon prints for Goose in the Pond block triangles and block centers

1 fat eighth *each* of 7 assorted dark-brown prints for Goose in the Pond block nine-patch units

1 fat eighth *each* of 7 assorted grayish-green prints for Goose in the Pond block nine-patch units

1 fat eighth *each* of 6 assorted dark-brown prints for Singe Irish Chain blocks

⅞ yard of cinnamon print for middle border and outer-border corner squares

⅔ yard of tan print for inner border

¼ yard of dark-brown print for outer-border corner squares

⅝ yard of fabric for binding

4¾ yards of fabric for backing

86" x 86" square of batting

GOOSE IN THE POND BLOCK CUTTING

Instructions are for cutting one pair of blocks. Before you begin cutting, make seven sets, with one cinnamon print, one dark-brown print, one grayish-green print, and one cream print in each set. Repeat these instructions for each set to make seven pairs of blocks (14 blocks total). Because you'll need only 13 blocks, refer to "Calculating the Cutting for a Single Block" on page 18 for how to cut one less block from the seventh set, if you don't want a leftover block. Cut the block sets separately in order to keep the prints in each set together.

From the dark-brown print, cut:
4 strips, 1¼" x 21"

From the grayish-green print, cut:
5 strips, 1¼" x 21"

From the cinnamon print, cut:
12 squares, 3¼" x 3¼"; cut in half diagonally to make 24 triangles
2 squares, 2¾" x 2¾"

From the cream print, cut:
12 squares, 3¼" x 3¼"; cut in half diagonally to make 24 triangles
8 squares, 2¾" x 2¾"

Pieced by Donna Lynn Thomas; machine quilted by Denise Mariano

SINGLE IRISH CHAIN BLOCK CUTTING

Instructions are for cutting one pair of blocks. Before you begin cutting, make six sets, with one dark-brown print and one cream print in each set. Repeat these instructions for each set to make six pairs of blocks (12 blocks total). Cut the block sets separately in order to keep the prints in each set together.

From the dark-brown print, cut:
3 strips, 1⅝" x 21"
2 squares, 2¾" x 2¾"

From the cream print, cut:
3 strips, 1⅝" x 21"
3 strips, 2¾" x 42"; crosscut into:
    16 squares, 2¾" x 2¾"
    8 rectangles, 2¾" x 5"

CUTTING FOR REMAINING PIECES

From the tan print, cut:
6 strips, 3½" x 42"

From the cinnamon print, cut:
7 strips, 2½" x 42"
1 strip, 6½" x 42"; crosscut into 4 squares,
    6½" x 6½"

From the dark-brown print, cut:
2 strips, 3½" x 42"; crosscut into 16 squares,
    3½" x 3½"

From the multicolored print, cut:
4 strips, 6½" x 80", from the *lengthwise grain* OR
8 strips, 6½" x 42", from the *crosswise grain*

From the binding fabric, cut:
8 strips, 2¼" x 42"

GOOSE IN THE POND BLOCK ASSEMBLY

Instructions are for making one pair of blocks at a time. Press all seam allowances in the direction of the arrows.

1. Select one set of Goose in the Pond block pieces. Join a dark-brown 1¼" x 21" strip to each long edge of a green 1¼" x 21" strip to make strip unit A. Crosscut the strip unit into 16 segments, 1¼" wide.

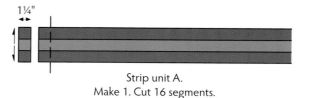

1¼"

Strip unit A.
Make 1. Cut 16 segments.

2. Join a green 1¼" x 21" strip to each long edge of a dark-brown 1¼" x 21" strip to make strip unit B. Repeat to make a total of two strip units. Crosscut the strip units into eight segments, 1¼" wide, and eight segments, 2¾" wide.

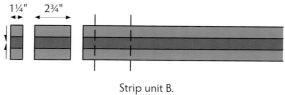

1¼"   2¾"

Strip unit B.
Make 2. Cut 8 segments, 1¼", and
8 segments, 2¾".

3. Sew two strip unit A segments and one 1¼"-wide strip unit B segment together as shown. Repeat to make a total of eight nine-patch units.

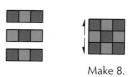

Make 8.

4. Sew a cinnamon 3¼" triangle to a cream 3¼" triangle along the long bias edges. Repeat to make a total of 24 half-square-triangle units. Press. Trim the units to 2¾" x 2¾".

Make 24.

5. Lay out 12 half-square-triangle units, four nine-patch units, four 2¾"-wide strip unit B segments, four cream 2¾" squares, and one cinnamon 2¾" square into five horizontal rows as shown. Sew the units in each row together. Join the rows to make a Goose in the Pond block. Repeat to make a second block.

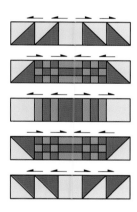

Make 2.

6. Repeat steps 1–5 with the remaining Goose in the Pond sets to make a total of 14 blocks. You'll have one extra block unless you followed the cutting instructions on pages 26 and 27 to cut one less block from the seventh set.

SINGLE IRISH CHAIN BLOCK ASSEMBLY

Instructions are for making one pair of blocks at a time. Press all seam allowances in the direction of the arrows.

1. Select one set of Single Irish Chain block pieces. Join a dark-brown 1⅝" x 21" strip to one long edge of a cream 1⅝" x 21" strip. Repeat to make a total of three strip sets.

Crosscut the strip sets into 32 segments, 1⅝" wide.

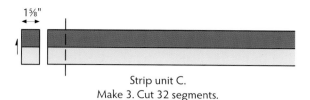

Strip unit C.
Make 3. Cut 32 segments.

2. Sew the segments into pairs as shown to make 16 four-patch units.

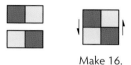

Make 16.

3. Sew two four-patch units and two cream 2¾" squares together as shown. Make eight double four-patch units.

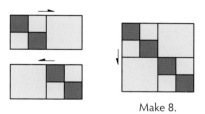

Make 8.

4. Lay out four double four-patch units, four cream rectangles, and one dark-brown 2¾" square into three horizontal rows as shown. Sew the units in each row together. Join the rows to make a Single Irish Chain block. Repeat to make a second block.

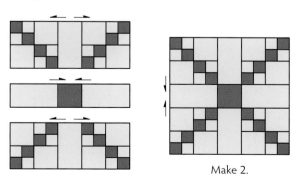

Make 2.

5. Repeat steps 1–4 with the remaining Single Irish Chain sets to make a total of 12 blocks.

QUILT-TOP ASSEMBLY

1. Refer to the quilt assembly diagram at right to lay out 13 Goose in the Pond blocks and the 12 Single Irish Chain blocks into a pleasing arrangement of five rows of five blocks each. The seams between blocks should butt nicely when the blocks are rotated a quarter turn. Sew the blocks in each row together. Join the rows to complete the center of the quilt.

2. Sew the tan 3½"-wide strips together end to end to make one long strip. From this pieced strip, measure and cut two strips to fit the center length of the quilt top. Sew these strips to the sides of the quilt top. From the remainder of the pieced strip, measure and cut two strips to fit the center width of the quilt top. Sew these strips to the top and bottom of the quilt top to complete the inner border.

3. Repeat step 2 with the cinnamon 2½"-wide strips to add the middle border to the quilt top.

4. Refer to "Folded Corners" on page 7 to draw a diagonal line on the wrong side of each dark-brown 3½" square. Sew marked squares to opposite corners of a cinnamon 6½" square. Trim ¼" from the stitching line and press the seam allowances toward the brown corners. Repeat for the remaining corners to make a square-within-a-square unit. Repeat to make a total of four outer-border corner squares.

Make 4.

5. If you cut 80"-long lengthwise-grain strips from the multicolored fabric, trim them to fit the center width and length of the quilt top, adjusting the strips as necessary before trimming so that the motifs are centered on each side of the quilt top. If you cut crosswise-grain strips, sew the strips into pairs, and then trim each pieced strip to fit the center width and length of the quilt top as described for the lengthwise-grain strips. Sew two strips to the sides of the quilt top. Sew the border corner squares to the ends of the remaining two strips, and sew these strips to the top and bottom of the quilt top to complete the outer border.

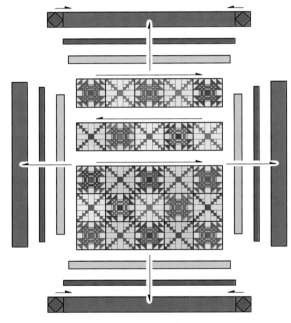

Quilt assembly

FINISHING

1. Layer the quilt top with batting and backing; baste the layers together.

2. Quilt as desired.

3. Bind the quilt edges with the 2¼"-wide binding strips.

Color Option

"Goose on Rainbow Pond," machine pieced by Ann Burgess
and machine quilted by Denise Mariano

Ann used a rainbow of batiks in her Goose in the Pond blocks. This gorgeous quilt is a Mixed recipe because she used one background print in all her Goose blocks and two different background prints in her Single Irish Chain blocks. The stunning border print was her color inspiration.

Candy Dots

These simple, pretty blocks are made one pair at a time using a set of dark, medium, and light prints from the same color family. Draw from many color families to make this cheery Rainbow-recipe quilt. The pieced border, which is really just an extension of the block design, is cut and sewn at the same time you make the blocks.

FINISHED QUILT: 60½" x 60½" • FINISHED BLOCK: 9" x 9" • Make 36 blocks.

SKILL LEVEL: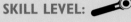

MATERIALS

Yardage is based on 42"-wide fabric.

1 fat eighth *each* of 18 assorted dark prints and 18 assorted light prints for blocks

1 fat quarter *each* of 18 assorted medium prints for blocks

⅝ yard of fabric for binding

4 yards of fabric for backing

68" x 68" square of batting

BLOCK CUTTING

Instructions are for cutting one pair of blocks. Before you begin cutting, make 18 sets, with one dark print, one medium print, and one light print in each set. Repeat these instructions for each set to make 18 pairs of blocks (36 blocks total). Cut the block sets separately in order to keep the prints in each set together. Appliqué pattern A is on page 35; determine your appliqué method before cutting the pieces.

From the dark print, cut:

5 squares, 4" x 4"; cut in half diagonally to make 10 triangles

3 squares, 2½" x 2½"; cut in half diagonally to make 6 triangles

6 of A

From the medium print, cut:

14 squares, 3½" x 3½"

3 squares, 2½" x 2½"; cut in half diagonally to make 6 triangles

From the light print, cut:

5 squares, 4" x 4"; cut in half diagonally to make 10 triangles

CUTTING FOR REMAINING PIECES

From the binding fabric, cut:

7 strips, 2¼" x 42"

BLOCK AND BORDER-UNIT ASSEMBLY

Instructions are for making one pair of blocks at a time, as well as the border units. Press all seam allowances in the direction of the arrows.

1. Select one set of block pieces. Sew a dark 4" triangle to a light 4" triangle along the long bias edges. Repeat to make a total of 10 half-square-triangle units. Press the seam allowances of five units toward the dark and the remaining five units toward the light. Trim each unit to 3½" x 3½". Set aside two units,

Machine pieced and appliquéd by Donna Lynn Thomas; machine quilted by Denise Mariano

one pressed in each direction, for the pieced border.

Make 5.   Make 5.

2. Sew a dark 2½" triangle to a medium 2½" triangle along the long bias edges. Repeat to make a total of six half-square-triangle units.

Make 6.

3. Draw a diagonal line on the wrong side of each half-square-triangle unit from step 2. With right sides together, place the marked unit on one corner of a medium 3½" square as shown. Sew on the diagonal line. Trim ¼" from the stitching line. Repeat to make a total of six pinwheel squares. Press the seam allowances of three pinwheel squares toward the half-square-triangle unit and the remaining three toward the medium square. Set aside two pinwheel squares for the pieced border, one pressed in each direction.

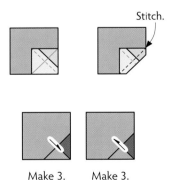

Stitch.

Make 3.   Make 3.

4. Lay out four half-square-triangle units from step 1 (two pressed in each direction), two pinwheel units from step 3 (one pressed in each direction), and three medium 3½" squares into three horizontal rows as shown.

Be careful to place the pressed seams in the correct positions. Sew the units in each row together. Join the rows to make a block. Repeat to make a second block.

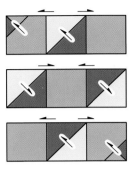 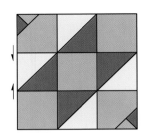

Make 2.

5. Using your preferred appliqué method, appliqué a dark circle to the center of each medium square in each block.

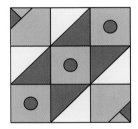

6. Repeat steps 1–5 with the remaining block sets to make a total of 36 blocks.

QUILT-TOP ASSEMBLY

1. Refer to the quilt assembly diagram on page 35 to lay out the blocks in six rows of six blocks each, balancing the colors throughout the quilt. Carefully orient the blocks as shown. Arrange the pressing directions of each block so that all seams will butt where the blocks meet. Sew the blocks in each row together. Join the rows to complete the center of the quilt.

2. Arrange 28 pinwheel squares, 24 medium 3½" squares, and 24 half-square-triangle units around the quilt center in a pleasing balance of color as shown in the diagram on page 35 and the photo on page 33. Arrange them so that units pressed in opposite directions sit next to each other. You'll have some leftover border units. Once you're pleased with the arrangement, sew the units into four border strips. Measure the side borders against the center length of the quilt top. If necessary, take in or let out small amounts of many seams to adjust the borders to fit. Sew these strips to the sides of the quilt center.

3. In the same manner, measure and adjust the top and bottom borders to fit the center width of the quilt top. Sew these strips to the quilt center.

FINISHING

1. Layer the quilt top with batting and backing; baste the layers together.
2. Quilt as desired.
3. Bind the quilt edges with the 2¼"-wide binding strips.

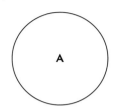

Pattern does not include seam allowance.

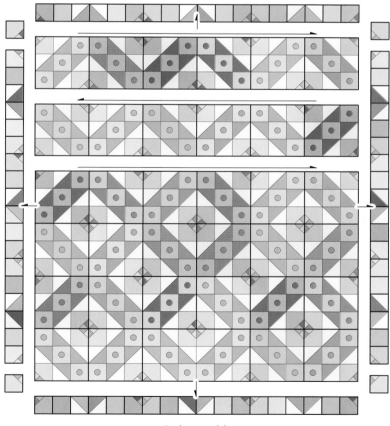

Quilt assembly

Color Option

*"A Touch of Americana," machine pieced and hand appliquéd
by Sally Malley and machine quilted by Kim Pope*

Sally's beautiful collection of blue and burgundy prints is so warm and comfortable in this Color Family–recipe quilt. Not only did she hand appliqué each of the circles, but she also pieced her binding using the prints from the body of the quilt.

Garden Glory

The beautiful Aster blocks in "Garden Glory" are made one pair at a time from a rainbow of colors, with the exception of the green prints that are assigned to the same position in all the blocks, making this a Mixed-recipe quilt. For each pair of blocks, choose a dark and a medium print in the same color family, an accent print, a green print, and a black background print. The blocks are tied together with a single green print that's used for the sashing squares and setting triangles, as well as a black solid fabric that appears in the sashing squares and outer border.

FINISHED QUILT: 63⅞" x 63⅞" • FINISHED BLOCK: 10" x 10" • Make 13 blocks.

SKILL LEVEL:

MATERIALS

Yardage is based on 42"-wide fabric.

⅝ yard *each* of 7 assorted black prints for block backgrounds and sashing strips

1⅛ yards of green print for sashing squares and setting triangles

⅞ yard of black solid for sashing squares and border

9" x 9" square *each* of 7 assorted dark prints for blocks

11" x 11" square *each* of 7 assorted medium prints for blocks

6" x 14" rectangle *each* of 7 assorted accent prints for blocks

8" x 13" rectangle *each* of 7 assorted green prints for blocks

⅝ yard of fabric for binding

4 yards of fabric for backing

70" x 70" square of batting

BLOCK CUTTING

Instructions are for cutting one pair of blocks. Before you begin cutting, make seven sets, with one dark print, one medium print, one accent print, one green print, and one black print in each set. Repeat the cutting instructions for each set to make seven pairs of blocks (14 blocks total). Because you'll need only 13 blocks, refer to "Calculating the Cutting for a Single Block" on page 18 for how to cut one less block from the seventh set, if you don't want a leftover block. Cut the block sets separately in order to keep the prints in each set together.

From the dark print, cut:
8 squares, 2½" x 2½"

From the medium print, cut:
4 squares, 4⅞" x 4⅞"; cut in half diagonally to make 8 half-square triangles

From the accent print, cut:
2 squares, 5¼" x 5¼"; cut into quarters diagonally to make 8 quarter-square triangles
2 squares, 2½" x 2½"

Continued on page 39.

Machine pieced by Donna Lynn Thomas; machine quilted by Pam Goggans

From the green print, cut:

4 squares, 3" x 3"; cut in half diagonally to make 8 half-square triangles

2 squares, 3¼" x 3¼"; cut into quarters diagonally to make 8 quarter-square triangles

From the black print, cut:

1 strip, 2½" x 42"; crosscut into 8 squares, 2½" x 2½"

1 strip, 3¼" x 42"; crosscut into:

    2 squares, 3¼" x 3¼"; cut into quarters diagonally to make 8 quarter-square triangles

    4 squares, 3" x 3"; cut in half diagonally to make 8 half-square triangles

    4 squares, 2⅞" x 2⅞"; cut in half diagonally to make 8 half-square triangles

CUTTING FOR REMAINING PIECES

From the remainder of the assorted black prints, cut a *total* of:

36 rectangles, 4½" x 10½"

From the green print, cut:

1 strip, 16" x 42"; crosscut into:

    2 squares, 16" x 16"; cut into quarters diagonally to make 8 large side setting triangles

1 strip, 4⅞" x 42"; crosscut into:

    6 squares, 4⅞" x 4⅞". Cut each square in half diagonally to make 12 small side setting triangles.

1 strip, 8½" x 42"; crosscut into:

    2 squares, 8½" x 8½"; cut in half diagonally to make 4 corner setting triangles

    24 squares, 2½" x 2½"

2 strips, 2½" x 42"; crosscut into 24 squares, 2½" x 2½"

From the black solid, cut:

7 strips, 2½" x 42"

2 strips, 4½" x 42"; crosscut into 12 squares, 4½" x 4½"

From the binding fabric, cut:

7 strips, 2¼" x 42"

BLOCK ASSEMBLY

Instructions are for making one pair of blocks at a time. Press all seam allowances in the direction of the arrows.

1. Refer to "Folded Corners" on page 7 to sew a dark 2½" square to the right-angle corner of a medium triangle. Trim ¼" from the stitching line. Repeat to make a total of eight striped triangles.

Make 8.

2. Sew a green 3¼" quarter-square triangle to a black 3¼" quarter-square triangle as shown. Repeat to make a total of eight pieced triangles.

Make 8.

3. Sew a pieced triangle to a black 2⅞" half-square triangle as shown. Repeat to make a total of eight triangle units.

Make 8.

4. Sew a triangle unit from step 3 to an accent 5¼" quarter-square triangle as shown. Repeat to make a total of eight units.

Make 8.

5. Sew a striped triangle from step 1 to a unit from step 4 as shown. Repeat to make a total of eight units.

Make 8.

6. Sew a green 3" half-square triangle to a black 3" half-square triangle. Press. Repeat to make a total of eight half-square-triangle units. Trim each unit to 2½" x 2½".

Make 8.

7. Sew a half-square-triangle unit from step 6 to a black 2½" square as shown. Make eight.

Make 8.

8. Sew a unit from step 5 to a unit from step 7 as shown. Repeat to make a total of eight flower units.

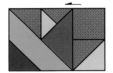

Make 8.

9. Partially sew an accent square to a flower unit from step 8, sewing only half of the seam as indicated by the dotted line. Leave the second half of the seam unstitched for now.

Partial seam

10. Sew a second flower unit to the left side of the unit from step 9. In the same fashion, sew a third and then a fourth flower unit in place, building on the previous unit as shown. As the final step, finish sewing the unstitched portion of the first seam.

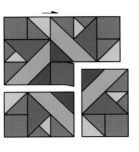 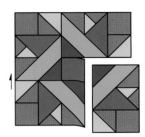

 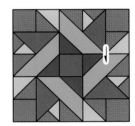

11. Repeat steps 9 and 10 to make a second block.

12. Repeat steps 1–11 with the remaining block sets to make a total of 14 blocks. You'll have one extra block when you assemble the quilt, unless you followed the cutting instructions on pages 37 and 39 to make one less block from the seventh set.

QUILT-TOP ASSEMBLY

1. Refer to "Folded Corners" on page 7 to draw a diagonal line on the wrong side of each green 2½" sashing square. Sew marked squares to opposite corners of a black solid 4½" square as shown. Trim ¼" from the stitching line and press the seam allowances toward the green corners. Repeat for the remaining corners to make a sashing square. Make a total of 12 sashing squares.

Make 12.

2. Refer to the quilt assembly diagram below to lay out 13 blocks, the 12 sashing squares, the assorted black print 4½" x 10½" sashing strips, the green large and small side setting triangles, and the green corner setting triangles in diagonal rows as shown. Sew the units in each row together. Join the rows. Add the corner setting triangles last. Trim the quilt top to ¼" from the sashing corner points.

3. Sew the black solid 2½"-wide strips together end to end to make one long strip. From this pieced strip, measure and cut two strips to fit the center length of the quilt top. Sew these strips to the sides of the quilt top. From the remainder of the pieced strip, measure and cut two strips to fit the center width of the quilt top. Sew these strips to the top and bottom of the quilt top.

FINISHING

1. Layer the quilt top with batting and backing; baste the layers together.

2. Quilt as desired.

3. Bind the quilt edges with the 2¼"-wide binding strips.

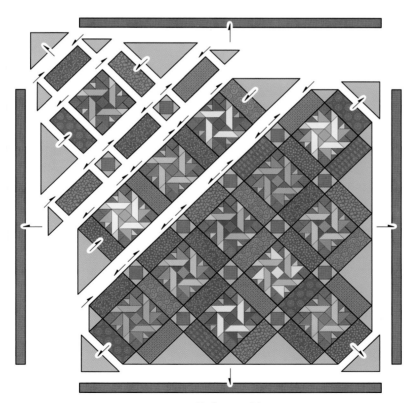

Quilt assembly

Color Option

"Hidden Stars," machine pieced by Nancy Wakefield and machine quilted by Denise Mariano

Nancy chose handwoven plaids for her Color Family–recipe quilt, giving this pattern a completely different look. It was easy to reduce the size of the main pattern by making the blocks one at a time. This comfy quilt is just beautiful!

When the Wind Blows

This happy 1930s reproduction quilt is a Mixed recipe. The 24 blocks are made one pair at a time from 12 sets of dark and medium prints in a rainbow of colors. The same cream print is used in all the blocks and borders, while the sawtooth border features leftovers from the blocks.

FINISHED QUILT: 60½" x 82½" • FINISHED BLOCK: 11" x 11" • Make 24 blocks.

SKILL LEVEL:

MATERIALS

Yardage is based on 42"-wide fabric.

6 yards of cream print for blocks and borders

1 fat quarter *each* of 12 dark prints for blocks and middle sawtooth border

11" x 21" rectangle *each* of 12 medium prints for blocks and middle sawtooth border

5" x 5" square *each* of 4 additional medium prints for outer-border corner squares

½ yard of fabric for binding

5 yards of fabric for backing

68" x 90" piece of batting

BLOCK CUTTING

Instructions are for cutting one pair of blocks. Before you begin cutting, make 12 sets, with one dark print and one medium print in each set. Keep the pieces in each set together as you cut them. Because each block uses the same background fabrics, cutting instructions for those pieces are given under "Cutting for Remaining Pieces."

From the dark print, cut:
2 squares, 3½" x 3½"
4 strips, 1½" x 21"

From the medium print, cut:
8 squares, 3½" x 3½"
8 squares, 2" x 2"

CUTTING FOR REMAINING PIECES

From the remainder of *each* of the 12 medium prints, cut:
1 square, 3" x 3"; cut in half diagonally to make 2 triangles (24 total)

From the remainder of 1 of the medium prints, cut:
1 square, 3" x 3"; cut in half diagonally to make 2 triangles

From the cream print, cut:
24 strips, 3½" x 42"; crosscut into:
    96 rectangles, 3½" x 4½"
    24 strips, 3½" x 21"
1 strip, 3" x 42"; crosscut into 13 squares, 3" x 3". Cut in half diagonally to make 26 triangles.
18 strips, 2½" x 42"; crosscut *12 of the strips* into 24 strips, 2½" x 21"
5 strips, 2" x 42"; crosscut into 96 squares, 2" x 2"
12 strips, 1½" x 42"; crosscut into 24 strips, 1½" x 21"
1 strip, 5" x 42"; crosscut into 4 squares, 5" x 5"
7 strips, 4½" x 42"

From the binding fabric, cut:
8 strips, 2¼" x 42"

Machine pieced and quilted by Katharine Brigham

BLOCK ASSEMBLY

Instructions are for making one pair of blocks at a time. Press all seam allowances in the direction of the arrows.

1. Select one set of dark and medium fabric pieces. Sew a dark 1½" x 21" strip to a cream 3½" x 21" strip along one long edge to make strip unit A. Repeat to make a total of two strip units. Crosscut the strip units into 16 segments, 1½" wide.

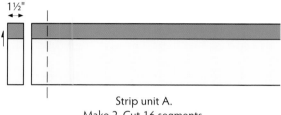

Strip unit A.
Make 2. Cut 16 segments.

2. Sew one of the remaining dark 1½" x 21" strips between a cream 1½" x 21" strip and a cream 2½" x 21" strip to make strip unit B. Repeat to make a total of two strip units. Crosscut the strip units into 16 segments, 1½" wide.

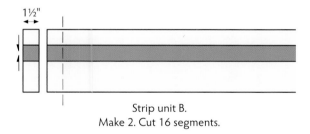

Strip unit B.
Make 2. Cut 16 segments.

3. Lay out two segments from step 1 and two segments from step 2 as shown. Sew the segments together to form a corner unit. Repeat to make a total of eight corner units.

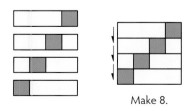

Make 8.

4. Refer to "Folded Corners" on page 7 to draw a diagonal line on the wrong side of the eight medium 3½" squares. Sew a marked square to one end of a cream 3½" x 4½" rectangle as shown. Trim ¼" from the stitching line. Reserve the trimmed-away triangles for the middle sawtooth border. Repeat to make a total of eight pieced rectangles.

Make 8.

5. Draw a diagonal line on the wrong side of eight cream 2" squares. Refer to "Folded Corners" to sew a marked square to the medium-print corner of a pieced rectangle from step 4 as shown. Trim ¼" from the stitching line. Repeat to make a total of eight striped rectangles.

Make 8.

6. Refer to "Folded Corners" to draw a diagonal line on the wrong side of the eight medium 2" squares. Sew marked squares to opposite corners of a dark 3½" square as shown. Trim ¼" from the stitching line and press the seam allowances toward the medium-print corners. Repeat for the remaining corners to make a block center unit. Make a total of two units.

Make 2.

7. Lay out four corner units, four striped rectangles, and one block center into three horizontal rows as shown. Sew the units in each row together. Join the rows to make a block. Repeat to make a second block.

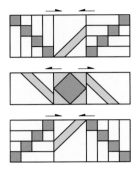 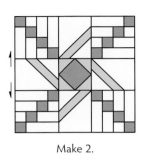

Make 2.

8. Repeat steps 1–7 with the remaining block sets to make a total of 24 blocks.

QUILT-TOP ASSEMBLY

1. Refer to the quilt assembly diagram on page 47 to lay out the blocks in six rows of four blocks each, rearranging them until you're pleased with the color placement through-out the quilt. Rotate the blocks one quarter so the seams butt from block to block. Sew the blocks in each row together. Join the rows to complete the quilt center.

2. Sew the remaining six cream 2½"-wide strips together end to end to make one long strip. From this pieced strip, measure and cut two strips to fit the center length of the quilt top. Sew these strips to the sides of the quilt top. From the remainder of the pieced strip, measure and cut two strips to fit the center width of the quilt top. Sew these strips to the top and bottom of the quilt top to complete the inner border.

3. Using the 96 reserved medium and cream trimmed-away triangles and the 26 medium and cream 3" triangles, make 122 half-square-triangle units as shown. Trim each unit to 2½" x 2½".

Make 122.

4. Randomly sew 35 half-square-triangle units together as shown. Repeat to make a total of two strips. Adjust the length of the border strips as needed to fit the center length of the quilt top, taking in or letting out a small amount of many seams. Sew the borders to the sides of the quilt top, being careful to orient the triangles correctly as shown in the quilt assembly diagram.

Side border.
Make 2.

5. In the same manner, randomly sew 24 half-square-triangle units together as shown. Repeat to make a total of two strips. Adjust the strips as needed to fit the center width of the quilt top. Sew the borders to the top and bottom of the quilt top, being careful to orient the triangles in the correct direction.

Top/bottom border.
Make 2.

6. To make the outer-border corner squares, refer to "Add-an-Inch Bias Squares" on page 6 and layer each medium 5" square with a cream 5" square, right sides together. Cut each pair in half diagonally and stitch the triangle pairs together along the long edges. Trim each unit to 4½" x 4½".

7. Sew the cream 4½"-wide strips together end to end to make one long strip. From this pieced strip, measure and cut two strips to fit the center length of the quilt top and two strips to fit the center width of the quilt top. Stitch the longer strips to the sides of the quilt top. Select four different corner squares from step 6 and sew them to both ends of each of the remaining two strips. You'll have four corner squares left over for another project. Join the strips to the top and bottom of the quilt top to complete the outer border.

FINISHING

1. Layer the quilt top with batting and backing; baste the layers together.
2. Quilt as desired.
3. Bind the quilt edges with the 2¼"-wide binding strips.

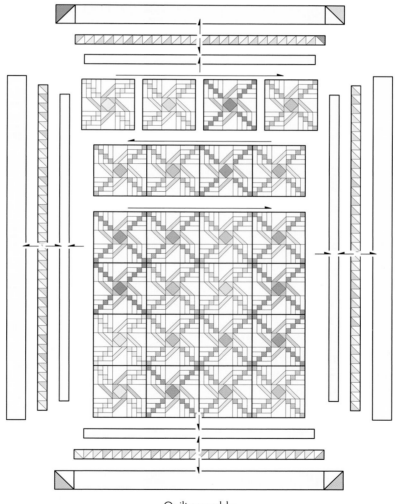

Quilt assembly

Color Option

"Fresh Breeze," machine pieced by Jeanne Poore and machine quilted by Theresa Ward; from the collection of Donna Lynn Thomas

This light-and-breezy Rainbow-recipe quilt is just as pretty in fresh contemporary prints. Each pair of blocks uses a different set of prints, including the background fabric. The cheerful print in the border served as color inspiration for the blocks.

Gems

This colorful quilt is a Mixed recipe because, although each set of blocks is made from a completely different color family (as in the Rainbow recipe), the same light background print is used in all the blocks. The blocks are made four at a time from 12 sets of dark and medium solids and the background print.

FINISHED QUILT: 54½" x 66½" • FINISHED BLOCK: 6" x 6" • Make 48 blocks.

SKILL LEVEL:

MATERIALS

Yardage is based on 42"-wide fabric.

1 fat quarter or ¼ yard *each* of 12 assorted dark solids for blocks and pieced middle border

3⅛ yards of white-on-white print for blocks, inner and outer borders, and binding

1 fat eighth *each* of 12 assorted medium solids for blocks and pieced middle border

3½ yards of fabric for backing (horizontal seam)

62" x 74" piece of batting

BLOCK CUTTING

Instructions are for cutting four blocks. Before you begin cutting, make 12 sets, with one dark solid and one medium solid in each set. Keep the pieces in each set together as you cut them. Because each block uses the same background fabrics, cutting instructions for those pieces are given under "Cutting for Remaining Pieces."

From the medium solid, cut:

8 squares, 3" x 3"; cut in half diagonally to make 16 triangles

8 squares, 1½" x 1½"

From the dark solid, cut:

4 squares, 3" x 3"; cut in half diagonally to make 8 triangles

8 squares, 2½" x 2½"

16 squares, 1½" x 1½"

CUTTING FOR REMAINING PIECES

From the white-on-white print, cut:

12 strips, 3" x 42"; crosscut into 144 squares, 3" x 3". Cut each square in half diagonally to make 288 triangles.

3 strips, 2½" x 42"; crosscut into 48 squares, 2½" x 2½"

5 strips, 3½" x 42"

6 strips, 4½" x 42"

6 strips, 2¼" x 42"

From the remainder of the medium and dark solids, cut a *total* of:

100 squares, 2½" x 2½" (4 or 5 from each solid)

Machine pieced by Donna Lynn Thomas; machine quilted by Denise Mariano

BLOCK ASSEMBLY

Instructions are for making one set of four blocks. Press all seam allowances in the direction of the arrows.

1. Select one set of medium and dark block pieces. Sew a medium 3" triangle to a white 3" triangle as shown. Make 16 medium/white half-square-triangle units. Press the seam allowances of eight units toward the medium triangle and the remaining eight toward the white triangle. Trim each unit to 2½" x 2½".

Make 8.   Make 8.

2. Repeat step 1 with the dark and white 3" triangles to make eight dark/white half-square-triangle units, pressing half of the seam allowances toward the dark triangle and the remaining half toward the white triangle. Trim each unit to 2½" x 2½".

Make 4.   Make 4.

3. Refer to "Folded Corners" on page 7 to draw a diagonal line on the wrong side of each dark 1½" square. Sew a marked square to the medium-fabric corner of each medium/white half-square-triangle unit from step 1 as shown. Trim ¼" from the stitching lines. Press each seam allowance in the same direction as the unit's previous seam allowances.

4. Repeat step 3 with the dark/white half-square triangle units from step 2 and the medium 1½" squares.

5. Lay out four medium/white striped squares from step 3, two dark/white striped squares from step 4, one white 2½" square, and two dark 2½" squares into three horizontal rows as shown. Be careful to orient the pressing directions of the striped squares as shown. Sew the units in each row together. Join the rows. Repeat to make a total of four blocks.

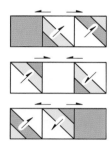 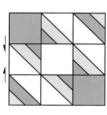

Make 4.

6. Repeat steps 1–5 with the remaining block sets to make a total of 48 blocks.

QUILT-TOP ASSEMBLY

1. Refer to the quilt assembly diagram on page 52 to lay out the blocks in eight rows of six blocks each, balancing the placement of colors across the surface of the quilt. Sew the blocks in each row together. Join the rows.

2. Sew the white 3½"-wide strips together end to end to make one long strip. From this pieced strip, measure and cut two strips to fit the center length of the quilt top. Sew these strips to the sides of the quilt top. From the remainder of the pieced strip, measure and cut two strips to fit the center width of the quilt top. Sew these strips to the top and bottom of the quilt top to complete the inner border.

3. Randomly sew 27 medium and dark 2½"
   squares together to make one long strip.
   Repeat to make a total of two strips. Sew
   these strips to the sides of the quilt top. In
   the same manner, randomly sew 23 medium
   and dark squares together. Repeat to make
   a total of two strips. Sew these strips to the
   top and bottom of the quilt top to complete
   the middle border.
4. Repeat step 2 with the white 4½"-wide strips
   to add the outer border to the quilt top.

FINISHING

1. Layer the quilt top with batting and backing;
   baste the layers together.
2. Quilt as desired.
3. Bind the quilt edges with the white 2¼"-
   wide binding strips.

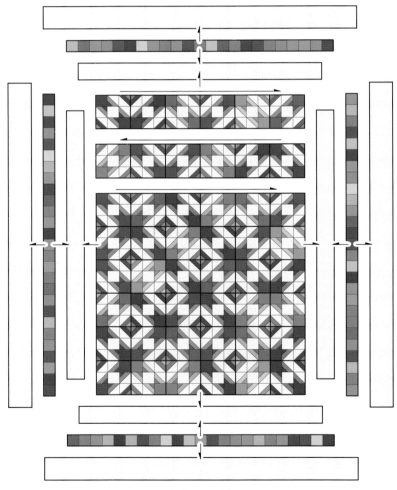

Quilt assembly

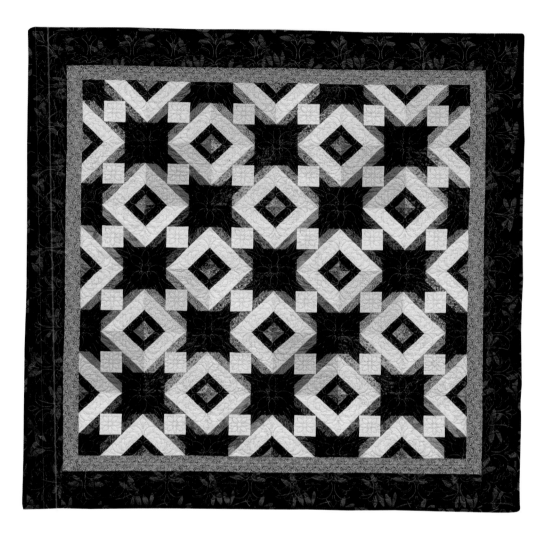

Color Option

*"Black Diamonds," machine pieced by Donna Lynn Thomas
and machine quilted by Denise Mariano*

Striking blacks and grays give this Color Family version of "Gems" a very graphic look. It's easy to increase the size of this quilt by making more block sets. This would be a great quilt for a young man.

Roses for My Love

This traditional pink-and-green appliqué quilt looks gorgeous on a queen-size bed. It's another lovely example of the Mixed recipe in action. All the Rose Wreath and Lily blocks are made one at a time from a set of dark-red, medium-red, dark-green, and medium-green prints. The Lily blocks each have a different background print, putting them within the Color Family recipe, while the Rose Wreath blocks are all appliquéd to the same background print, making them a Mixed recipe.

FINISHED QUILT: 90⅜" x 90⅜" • FINISHED BLOCK: 16" x 16"
Make 9 Lily blocks and 4 Rose Wreath blocks.

SKILL LEVEL:

MATERIALS

Yardage is based on 42"-wide fabric.

1 fat quarter *each* of 9 assorted light prints for Lily blocks

2⅛ yards of pink-and-green print for fourth border

1 fat eighth *each* of 13 assorted dark-green, 13 assorted medium-green, 13 assorted dark-red, and 13 assorted medium-red prints for blocks

1½ yards of medium-pink print for first and third borders and binding

1½ yards of light-pink print for setting triangles

1⅛ yards of medium-light print for Rose Wreath block backgrounds

⅔ yard of light-green print for second border

9 yards of fabric for backing

98" x 98" square of batting

LILY BLOCK CUTTING

Instructions are for cutting one block. Before you begin cutting, make nine sets, with one dark-green print, one medium-green print, one dark-red print, one medium-red print, and one light print in each set. Repeat the cutting instructions for each set to make nine blocks. Cut the block sets separately in order to keep the prints in each set together. Appliqué patterns I and J are on page 61; determine your appliqué method before cutting the pieces.

From the medium-green print, cut:
8 squares, 2½" x 2½"
4 of J

From the dark-green print, cut:
8 squares, 2½" x 2½"
1 strip, ⅞" x 13"
2 strips, ⅞" x 6½"
8 of I

Continued on page 56.

Machine pieced and appliquéd by Carol Kirchhoff; machine quilted by Freda Smith

From the light print, cut:
1 square, 8¾" x 8¾"; cut into quarters diagonally to make 4 triangles
16 squares, 2½" x 2½"
4 squares, 4½" x 4½"
2 squares, 3" x 3"; cut in half diagonally to make 4 triangles

From the dark-red print, cut:
8 rectangles, 2½" x 4½"

From the medium-red print, cut:
4 rectangles, 2½" x 4½"
2 squares, 3" x 3"; cut in half diagonally to make 4 triangles

ROSE WREATH BLOCK CUTTING

Instructions are for cutting one block. Before you begin cutting, make four sets, with one dark-green print, one medium-green print, one dark-red print, and one medium-red print in each set. Repeat the cutting instructions for each set to make four blocks. Cut the block sets separately in order to keep the prints in each set together. Because each block uses the same background fabric, the total number of squares needed from the medium-light fabric is also given so that you can either cut all the squares at once, or cut them one at a time as you cut the other pieces in each set. Appliqué patterns A–H are on page 61; determine your appliqué method before cutting the pieces.

From the dark-green print, cut:
8 of B
4 of H

From the medium-green print, cut:
16 of A

From the dark-red print, cut:
8 of C
1 of D
1 of F

From the medium-red print, cut:
1 of E
8 of G

From the medium-light print, cut:
1 square, 17½" x 17½" (or 4 squares total)

CUTTING FOR REMAINING PIECES

From the light-pink print, cut:
2 squares, 24½" x 24½"; cut into quarters diagonally to make 8 side setting triangles
2 squares, 13" x 13"; cut in half diagonally to make 4 corner setting triangles

From the medium-pink print, cut:
16 strips, 1½" x 42"
10 strips, 2¼" x 42"

From the light-green print, cut:
8 strips, 2½" x 42"

From the pink-and-green print, cut:
9 strips, 7½" x 42"

LILY BLOCK ASSEMBLY

Instructions are for making one block at a time. Press all seam allowances in the direction of the arrows.

1. Select one set of Lily block pieces. Using your favorite appliqué method, prepare and appliqué a J stem and two I leaves to a light triangle as shown. Repeat to make a total of four appliquéd triangles.

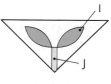

Make 4.

2. Sew units from step 1 to the long sides of a dark-green ⅞" x 6½" strip as shown. Repeat to make a total of two units.

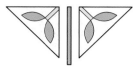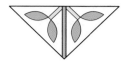

Make 2.

3. Sew the units from step 2 to the long edges of the dark-green ⅞" x 13" strip, centering and aligning the shorter green strips so they align on opposite sides of the center strip. Trim the block center to 8½" x 8½", keeping the dark-green strips centered on the square.

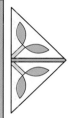

4. Refer to "Folded Corners" on page 7 to draw a diagonal line on the wrong side of each medium-green 2½" square. Sew a marked square to one corner of a light 4½" square as shown. Trim ¼" from the stitching line. Press. Repeat on the adjacent corner. Repeat to make a total of four units.

Make 4.

5. Draw a diagonal line on the wrong side of eight light 2½" squares. Sew a marked square to one end of each dark-red 2½" x 4½" rectangle, orienting four in one direction and four in the opposite direction as shown. Trim ¼" from the stitching lines.

Make 4.

Make 4.

6. Draw a diagonal line on the wrong side of each dark-green 2½" square. Sew a marked square to the opposite end of each unit from step 5, orienting the squares in the same direction as the previous squares to make striped rectangles. Trim ¼" from the stitching lines.

Make 4.

Make 4.

7. Sew one of each striped rectangle from step 6 to the sides of a unit from step 4 as shown. Butt diagonal seams when sewing for sharp points. Repeat to make a total of four side units.

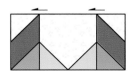

Make 4.

8. Refer to "Folded Corners" to mark and sew a light 2½" square to one end of a medium-red 2½" x 4½" rectangle as shown. Trim ¼" from the stitching line. Repeat to make a total of four units.

Make 4.

9. Sew a light 3" triangle to a medium-red 3" triangle along the long bias edges. Repeat to make a total of four half-square-triangle units. Press. Trim the units to 2½" x 2½".

Make 4.

10. Sew a half-square-triangle unit from step 9 to a light 2½" square. Repeat to make a total of four units.

Make 4.

11. Sew a unit from step 10 to a unit from step 8 as shown. Repeat to make a total of four block corners.

Make 4.

12. Lay out the appliquéd block center, the four corner units, and the four side units into three horizontal rows as shown. Sew the units in each row together. Join the rows.

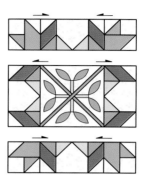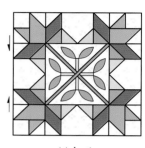

Make 1.

13. Repeat steps 1–12 with the remaining block sets to make a total of nine Lily blocks.

ROSE WREATH BLOCK ASSEMBLY

Instructions are for making one block at a time. Press all seam allowances in the direction of the arrows.

1. Select one set of Rose Wreath block pieces. Fold the medium-light background square in half vertically, horizontally, and diagonally and finger-press the folds to create centering guides for your appliqué pieces.

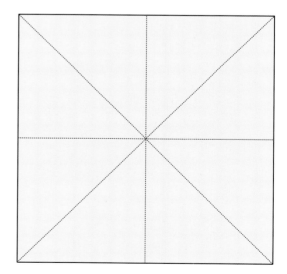

2. Using a chalk pencil or air- or water-soluble marking pen and the appliqué placement guide below, mark the pattern on each quarter of the background square.

3. Using your preferred appliqué method, prepare and appliqué pieces A–H to the background square, beginning with the stems, followed by the rosebuds and leaves, and finally the layers of the center rose.

Appliqué placement

4. Trim the appliquéd block to 16½" x 16½", keeping the design centered.

5. Repeat steps 1–4 with the remaining block sets to make a total of four Rose Wreath blocks.

QUILT-TOP ASSEMBLY

1. Refer to the quilt assembly diagram on page 60 to lay out the blocks and the light-pink side and corner setting triangles in diagonal rows as shown. Sew the blocks and side setting triangles in each diagonal row together. Join the rows. Add the corner setting triangles last. Trim the quilt top to ¼" from the block points.

2. Sew the medium-pink 1½"-wide strips together end to end to make one long strip. From this pieced strip, measure and cut two strips to fit the center length of the quilt top. Sew these strips to the sides of the quilt top. From the remainder of the pieced strip, measure and cut two strips to fit the center width of the quilt top. Sew these strips to the top and bottom of the quilt top to complete the first border. Set aside the remainder of the strip for the third border.

3. Repeat step 2 with the light-green 2½"-wide strips to add the second border to the quilt top. Use the remainder of the pieced medium-pink strip to add the third border to the quilt top, followed by the pink-and-green 7½"-wide strips for the fourth border.

FINISHING

1. Layer the quilt top with batting and backing; baste the layers together.
2. Quilt as desired.
3. Bind the quilt edges with the medium-pink 2¼"-wide binding strips.

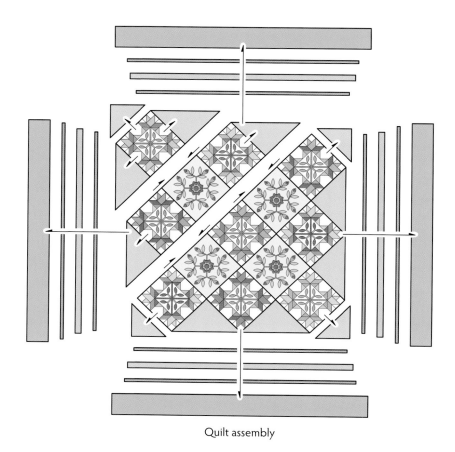

Quilt assembly

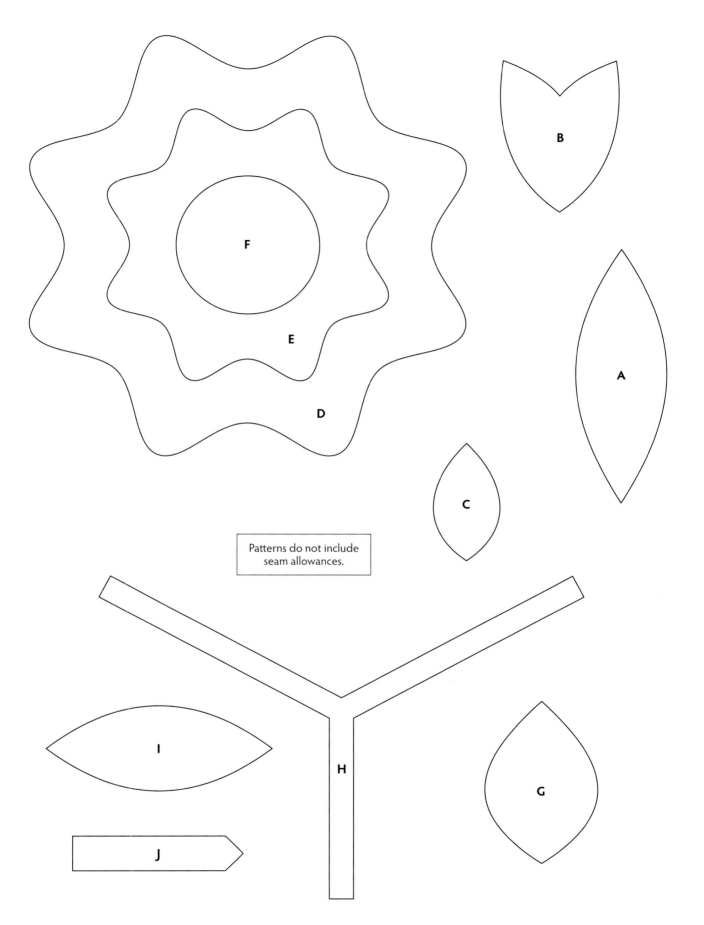

Patterns do not include seam allowances.

Appliqué placement guide

Color Option

*"Chartreuse Masquerade," machine pieced, hand appliquéd,
and machine quilted by Linda Kittle*

This quilt could not be more different from "Roses for My Love"! Linda always has a fun, contemporary take on the traditional, and this time she took her inspiration from the border print. See if you can find the Mardi Gras masks that Linda's husband, Paul, detects in this quilt.

Delft Baskets

This pretty wall hanging, all in monochromatic blue, was inspired by a beautiful reproduction Dutch chintz I found online and used in the border. Having been to the Netherlands, the Delft factory, and the beautiful tulip gardens, and having a huge 30-plus year stash full of blue prints, I knew I had to make an all-blue quilt. Each Basket block is made from its own set of dark, medium, medium-light, and background prints. The Tulip blocks are made from two blue prints and a background print.

FINISHED QUILT: 42½" x 42½" • FINISHED BLOCK: 6" x 6"
Make 9 Basket blocks and 4 Tulip blocks.

SKILL LEVEL:

MATERIALS

Yardage is based on 42"-wide fabric.

1¼ yards of floral-striped fabric for inner border

10" x 10" square *each* of 13 assorted light background prints for blocks

5" x 21" rectangle *each* of 9 assorted medium-light-blue prints for blocks and sashing strips

8" x 8" square *each* of 13 assorted dark-blue prints for blocks and sashing squares

½ yard of dark-blue print for outer border

½ yard of medium-dark-blue floral for setting triangles

5" x 5" square *each* of 13 assorted medium-blue prints for blocks

½ yard of fabric for binding

2¾ yards of fabric for backing

48" x 48" square of batting

BASKET BLOCK CUTTING

Instructions are for cutting one block. Before you begin cutting, make nine sets, with one dark-blue print, one medium-blue print, one medium-light-blue print, and one light background print in each set. Repeat the cutting instructions for each set to make nine blocks. Cut the block sets separately in order to keep the prints in each set together.

From the medium-blue print, cut:
1 square, 2½" x 2½"; cut in half diagonally to make 2 triangles
1 square, 2" x 2"

From the light background print, cut:
1 square, 3⅞" x 3⅞"; cut in half diagonally to make 2 triangles (you'll have 1 left over)
1 square, 2½" x 2½"; cut in half diagonally to make 2 triangles
2 rectangles, 2" x 3½"
3 squares, 2" x 2"

From the dark-blue print, cut:
1 square, 2⅜" x 2⅜"; cut in half diagonally to make 2 triangles
3 squares, 2" x 2"

From the medium-light-blue print, cut:
2 rectangles, 2" x 3½"

Continued on page 66.

Machine pieced and appliquéd by Donna Lynn Thomas; machine quilted by Theresa Ward

TULIP BLOCK CUTTING

Instructions are for cutting one block. Before you begin cutting, make four sets, with one dark-blue print, one medium-blue print, and one light background print in each set. Repeat the cutting instructions for each set to make four blocks. Cut the block sets separately in order to keep the prints in each set together. Appliqué patterns A–C are on page 68; determine your appliqué method before cutting the pieces.

From the light background print, cut:
1 square, 7" x 7"

From the dark-blue print, cut:
4 of A
1 of C

From the medium-blue print, cut:
4 of B
4 of B reversed

CUTTING FOR REMAINING PIECES

From the remainder of the 9 assorted medium-light-blue prints, cut a *total* of:
36 strips, 1¾" x 6½"

From the remainder of the 13 assorted dark-blue prints, cut a *total* of:
24 squares, 1¾" x 1¾"

From the medium-dark-blue floral, cut:
2 squares, 12" x 12"; cut into quarters diagonally to make 8 side setting triangles
2 squares, 7½" x 7½"; cut in half diagonally to make 4 corner setting triangles

From the *lengthwise grain* of the floral-striped fabric, cut:
4 strips, 2¼" x 38"

From the dark-blue print for outer border, cut:
4 strips, 3½" x 42"

From the binding fabric, cut:
5 strips, 2¼" x 42"

BASKET BLOCK ASSEMBLY

Instructions are for making one block at a time. Press all seam allowances in the direction of the arrows.

1. Select one set of Basket block pieces. Sew a medium-blue 2½" triangle to a light background 2½" triangle along the long bias edges. Repeat to make a total of two half-square-triangle units. Press. Trim the units to 2" x 2".

Make 2.

2. Sew the two half-square-triangle units, the medium-blue 2" square, and a light background 2" square together as shown to make a corner unit. Release the stitching in the seam allowance of the center seam so that the seam allowances can be pressed in a clockwise direction.

Make 1.

3. Refer to "Folded Corners" on page 7 to draw a diagonal line on the wrong side of the two dark-blue and two light background 2" squares. Sew a marked dark square to one end of a medium-light-blue 2" x 3½" rectangle as shown (above right). Trim ¼" from the stitching line and press the seam allowances toward the dark-blue triangle. Repeat on the opposite corner with the light

square to make a flying-geese unit. Make one additional flying-geese unit, reversing the placement of the dark and light squares.

Make 1.   Make 1.

4. Sew a dark-blue 2⅜" triangle to one end of a light background 2" x 3½" rectangle as shown. Repeat to make a mirror-image unit.

Make 1.   Make 1.

5. Using the units from steps 2, 3, and 4, along with a light background 3⅞" triangle and the remaining dark-blue 2" square, assemble a Basket block as shown.

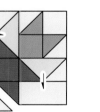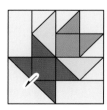

6. Repeat steps 1–5 with the remaining block sets to make a total of nine Basket blocks.

TULIP BLOCK ASSEMBLY

Instructions are for making one block at a time. Press all seam allowances in the direction of the arrows.

1. Select one set of Tulip block pieces. Fold the background square in half vertically, horizontally, and diagonally and finger-press the folds to create centering guides for your appliqué pieces.

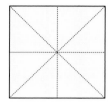

2. Using your preferred appliqué method and referring to the placement diagram below, prepare and appliqué pieces A–C to the background square.

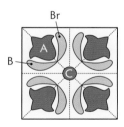
Appliqué placement

3. Trim the block to 6½" x 6½", keeping the design centered.
4. Repeat steps 1–3 with the remaining block sets to make a total of four Tulip blocks.

QUILT-TOP ASSEMBLY

1. Refer to the quilt assembly diagram on page 68 to lay out the blocks, the medium-light-blue 1¾" x 6½" sashing strips, the dark-blue 1¾" sashing squares, and the floral side and corner setting triangles into a pleasing arrangement of diagonal rows as shown. Sew the units together in each diagonal row. Join the rows. Add the corner setting

triangles last. Trim the quilt top ¼" from the sashing square corners.

2. Measure the length of the quilt top through the center and trim two floral inner-border strips to that measurement, positioning the motifs to fall on the edge of the quilt where you'd like them. Sew these strips to the sides of the quilt top. Measure the width of the quilt top through the center and trim the remaining two inner-border strips to this length, again positioning the motifs to fall as you wish. Sew these strips to the top and bottom of the quilt top.

3. Sew the dark-blue 3½"-wide strips together end to end to make one long strip. From this pieced strip, measure and cut two strips to fit the center length of the quilt top. Sew these strips to the sides of the quilt top. From the remainder of the pieced strip, measure and cut two strips to fit the center width of the quilt top. Sew these strips to the top and bottom of the quilt top to complete the outer border.

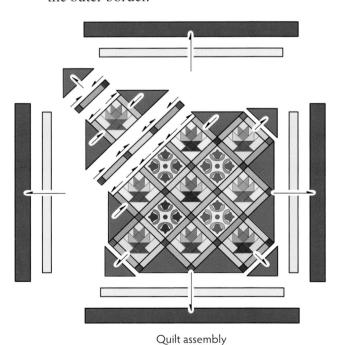

Quilt assembly

FINISHING

1. Layer the quilt top with batting and backing; baste the layers together.
2. Quilt as desired.
3. Bind the quilt edges with the 2¼"-wide binding strips.

Patterns do not include seam allowances.

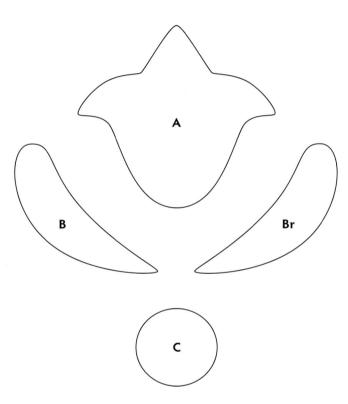

Color Option

"Pink Posies for Charlotte," machine pieced by Donna Lynn Thomas and machine quilted by Denise Mariano; from the collection of Charlotte Thomas

This pretty little wall hanging, made for my granddaughter, Charlotte, is a Mixed recipe. Opting to omit the Tulip blocks, I made the Basket blocks mostly from a Color Family recipe. The exception is the pots, which are all cut from the same pink print used in the border.

Starry Splendor

This lovely bed runner is made one pair of blocks at a time from six sets of prints. The black, red, green, and pink prints change with each pair of blocks as in a Color Family recipe, but what makes this quilt a Mixed recipe is the consistent use of the single tan print and single light background print throughout all the blocks. Start with a beautiful multicolored print for the outer border and pull your block fabrics from its colors.

FINISHED QUILT: 39½" x 87½" • FINISHED BLOCK: 12" x 12" • Make 12 blocks.

SKILL LEVEL:

MATERIALS

Yardage is based on 42"-wide fabric.

1 fat quarter *each* of 6 assorted black prints for blocks

1⅓ yards of light print for blocks and inner border

10" x 10" square *each* of 6 assorted green prints and 6 assorted pink prints for blocks

¼ yard *each* of 6 assorted red prints for blocks

⅞ yard of multicolored print for outer border

½ yard of red print for middle border

⅓ yard of tan print for blocks

⅝ yard of fabric for binding

4 yards of fabric for backing (horizontal seams)*

43" x 92" piece of batting

*If your usable fabric width is at least 43", 3 yards will be sufficient.

BLOCK CUTTING

Instructions are for cutting one pair of blocks. Before you begin cutting, make six sets, with one assorted black print, one assorted red print, one assorted green print, and one assorted pink print in each set. Repeat the cutting instructions for each set to make six pairs of blocks (12 blocks total). Cut the block sets separately in order to keep the pieces in each set together. Because each block uses the same background fabrics, cutting instructions for those pieces are given under "Cutting for Remaining Pieces" on page 72.

From the green print, cut:
8 squares, 3" x 3"; cut in half diagonally to make 16 triangles

From the pink print, cut:
8 squares, 2½" x 2½"

From the black print, cut:
2 squares, 4½" x 4½"
16 squares, 2½" x 2½"

From the red print, cut:
16 rectangles, 2½" x 4½"

Continued on page 72.

Machine pieced by Donna Lynn Thomas; machine quilted by Alice Scott

CUTTING FOR REMAINING PIECES

From the light print, cut:
6 strips, 2½" x 42"; crosscut into 96 squares,
    2½" x 2½"
4 strips, 3" x 42"; crosscut into 48 squares, 3" x 3".
    Cut each square in half diagonally to make 96
    triangles.
6 strips, 2½" x 42"

From the tan print, cut:
3 strips, 2½" x 42"; crosscut into 48 squares,
    2½" x 2½"

From the red print for middle border, cut:
6 strips, 2" x 42"

From the multicolored print, cut:
6 strips, 4½" x 42"

From the binding fabric, cut:
7 strips, 2¼" x 42"

BLOCK ASSEMBLY

Instructions are for making one pair of blocks at
a time. Press all seam allowances in the direction
of the arrows.

1. Select one set of block pieces. Sew a green 3"
   triangle to a light 3" triangle along the long
   bias edges. Repeat to make a total of 16 half-
   square-triangle units. Press the seam allowances of eight units toward the light triangle
   and the remaining eight units toward the
   green triangle. Trim the units to 2½" x 2½".

Make 8.   Make 8.

2. Arrange one half-square-triangle unit
   pressed in each direction, one tan 2½"
   square, and one pink 2½" square into two
   rows as shown. Sew the units in each row
   together. Join the rows. Release the stitching
   in the seam allowance of the final seam so
   that the seam allowances can be pressed in a

counterclockwise direction. Repeat to make
a total of eight corner units.

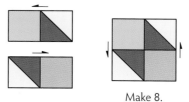

Make 8.

3. Refer to "Folded Corners" on page 7 to
   draw a diagonal line on the wrong side of
   each black 2½" square and 16 light 2½"
   squares. Sew a marked black square to one
   end of each red 2½" x 4½" rectangle, orienting eight in one direction and eight in the
   opposite direction as shown. Trim ¼" from
   the stitching line. Sew a marked light square
   to the opposite end of each rectangle, orienting the squares in the same direction as
   the previous squares to make eight striped
   rectangles and eight mirror-image striped
   rectangles. Trim ¼" from the stitching lines.

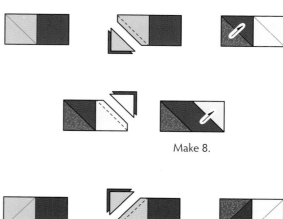

Make 8.

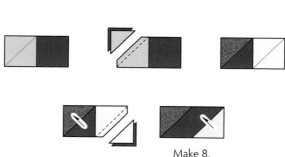

Make 8.

4. Sew a striped rectangle and a mirror-image striped rectangle together as shown. Repeat to make a total of eight chevron units.

Make 8.

5. Lay out four corner units, four chevron units, and a black 4½" square into three horizontal rows as shown. Sew the units in each row together. Join the rows. Repeat to make a second block.

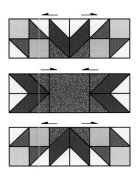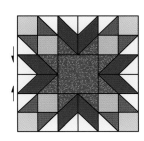

Make 2.

6. Repeat steps 1–5 with the remaining block sets to make a total of 12 blocks.

QUILT-TOP ASSEMBLY

1. Refer to the quilt assembly diagram at right to lay out the blocks in six rows of two blocks each, balancing the prints across the surface of the quilt. Sew the blocks in each row together. Join the rows.

2. Sew the light 2½"-wide strips together end to end to make one long strip. From this pieced strip, measure and cut two strips to fit the center length of the quilt top. Sew these strips to the sides of the quilt top. From the remainder of the pieced strip, measure and cut two strips to fit the center width of the quilt top. Sew these strips to the top and bottom of the quilt top to complete the inner border.

3. Repeat step 2 with the red 2"-wide strips to add the middle border and the multicolored 4½"-wide strips for the outer border.

Quilt assembly

FINISHING

1. Layer the quilt top with batting and backing; baste the layers together.

2. Quilt as desired.

3. Bind the quilt edges with the 2¼"-wide binding strips.

Color Option

*"Turquoise Nights," machine pieced by Donna Lynn Thomas
and machine quilted by Sandy Gore*

This richly hued Color Family–recipe quilt is set off by a border
composed of an extra seven chevron units made when sewing each
pair of blocks. The beautiful border print was the inspiration for
the colors in this quilt.

Carrie's Box

This wonderful red-and-white quilt, a Color Family recipe, relies on value to create the three-dimensional look of a folding box. Both the Folded Box blocks and the Carrie Nation blocks are made one pair at a time from different sets of dark-, medium-, and light-red prints on light background prints.

FINISHED QUILT: 80½" x 80½" • FINISHED BLOCK: 12" x 12"
Make 13 Folded Box blocks and 12 Carrie Nation blocks.

SKILL LEVEL:

MATERIALS

Yardage is based on 42"-wide fabric.

⅜ yard *each* of 6 light background prints for Carrie Nation blocks

2⅛ yards of cream print for second and fourth borders

1 fat quarter *each* of 7 light background prints for Folded Box blocks

1 fat quarter *each* of 7 dark-red prints for Folded Box blocks

1⅓ yards of red print for first border, third border, and binding

1 fat eighth *each* of 7 medium-red prints for Folded Box blocks

1 fat eighth *each* of 7 light-red prints for Folded Box blocks

1 fat eighth *each* of 6 dark-red prints for Carrie Nation blocks

1 fat eighth *each* of 6 light-red prints for Carrie Nation blocks

7⅓ yards of fabric for backing

88" x 88" square of batting

FOLDED BOX BLOCK CUTTING

Instructions are for cutting one pair of blocks. Before you begin cutting, make seven sets, with one dark-red print, one medium-red print, one light-red print, and one light background print in each set. Repeat these instructions for each set to make seven pairs of blocks (14 blocks total). Because you will need only 13 blocks, refer to "Calculating the Cutting for a Single Block" on page 18 for how to cut one less block from the seventh set, if you don't want a leftover block. Cut the block sets separately in order to keep the prints in each set together.

From the dark-red print, cut:
16 squares, 2½" x 2½"
2 squares, 4½" x 4½"

From the light background print, cut:
8 rectangles, 2½" x 4½"
8 squares, 2⅞" x 2⅞"; cut in half diagonally to make 16 triangles

From the light-red print, cut:
8 rectangles, 2½" x 4½"

From the medium-red print, cut:
4 squares, 4⅞" x 4⅞"; cut in half diagonally to make 8 triangles
8 squares, 2½" x 2½"

Continued on page 77.

Machine pieced by Donna Lynn Thomas; machine quilted by Sandy Gore

CARRIE NATION BLOCK CUTTING

Instructions are for cutting one pair of blocks. Before you begin cutting, make six sets, with one dark-red print, one light-red print, and one light background print in each set. Repeat these instructions for each set to make six pairs of blocks (12 blocks total). Cut the block sets separately in order to keep the prints in each set together.

From the dark-red print, cut:
2 strips, 2" x 20"

From the background print, cut:
2 strips, 2" x 20"
2 strips, 3½" x 16"
8 squares, 3½" x 3½"

From the light-red print, cut:
2 strips, 3½" x 16"

CUTTING FOR REMAINING PIECES

From the red print for first border, third border, and binding, cut:
14 strips, 1½" x 42"
9 strips, 2¼" x 42"

From the cream print, cut:
15 strips, 4½" x 42"

FOLDED BOX BLOCK ASSEMBLY

Instructions are for making one pair of blocks at a time. Press all seam allowances in the direction of the arrows.

1. Select one set of Folded Box block pieces. Refer to "Folded Corners" on page 7 to draw a diagonal line on the wrong side of each dark-red 2½" square. Sew a marked square to one end of a light background 2½" x 4½" rectangle as shown. Trim ¼" from the stitching line and press the seam allowances toward the dark-red triangle. Repeat on the opposite corner to make a

flying-geese unit. Repeat to make a total of eight flying-geese units.

Make 8.

2. Sew each unit from step 1 to a light-red rectangle as shown.

Make 8.

3. Sew light background triangles to adjacent sides of a medium-red 2½" square as shown. Repeat to make a total of eight units. Sew a medium-red 4⅞" triangle to each of these units as shown to make eight corner units.

Make 8.

4. Arrange four flying-geese units, four corner units, and a dark-red 4½" square into three horizontal rows as shown. Sew the units in each row together. Join the rows. Repeat to make a second block.

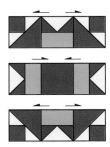
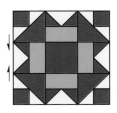

Make 2.

5. Repeat steps 1–4 with the remaining block sets to make a total of 14 blocks. You'll have one extra block when you assemble the quilt, unless you followed the cutting instructions on page 75 to make one less block from the seventh set.

CARRIE NATION BLOCK ASSEMBLY

Instructions are for making one pair of blocks at a time. Press all seam allowances in the direction of the arrows.

1. Select one set of Carrie Nation block pieces. Sew a dark-red 2" x 20" strip to a background 2" x 20" strip along the long edges to make strip unit A. Repeat to make a total of two strip units. Crosscut the strip units into 16 segments, 2" wide.

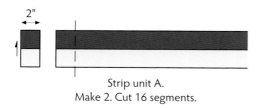

Strip unit A.
Make 2. Cut 16 segments.

2. Sew two strip unit A segments together as shown to make a four-patch unit. Repeat to make a total of eight four-patch units.

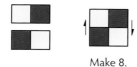

Make 8.

3. Lay out two four-patch units and two light background 3½" squares in two horizontal rows as shown. Sew the units in each row together. Join the rows. Release the stitching in the seam allowance of the final seam so that the seam allowances can be pressed in a

counterclockwise direction. Repeat to make a total of four double four-patch units.

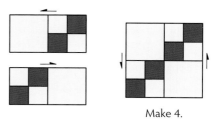

Make 4.

4. Sew a light-red 3½" x 16" strip to a light background 3½" x 16" strip along the long edges to make strip unit B. Repeat to make a total of two strip units. Crosscut the strip units into eight segments, 3½" wide.

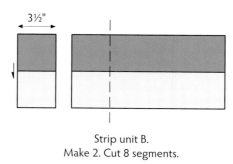

Strip unit B.
Make 2. Cut 8 segments.

5. Repeat step 2 with the strip unit B segments to make four four-patch units.

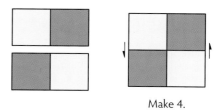

Make 4.

6. Arrange two double four-patch units from step 3 and two four-patch units from step 5 into two horizontal rows as shown. Sew the units in each row together. Join the rows. Repeat to make a second block.

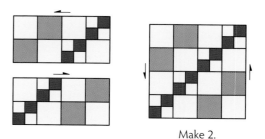

Make 2.

7. Repeat steps 1–6 with the remaining block sets to make a total of 12 Carrie Nation blocks.

QUILT-TOP ASSEMBLY

1. Refer to the quilt assembly diagram below to lay out 13 Folded Box blocks and the 12 Carrie Nation blocks into a pleasing arrangement of five rows of five blocks each, alternating the blocks in each row and from row to row. Sew the blocks in each row together. Join the rows.

2. Sew the red-print 1½"-wide strips together end to end to make one long strip. From this pieced strip, measure and cut two strips to fit the center length of the quilt top. Sew these strips to the sides of the quilt top. From the remainder of the pieced strip, measure and cut two strips to fit the center width of the quilt top. Sew these strips to the top and bottom of the quilt top to complete the first border. Set aside the remainder of the pieced strip for the third border.

3. Repeat step 2 with the cream 4½"-wide strips to add the second border to the quilt top. Use the remainder of the pieced red-print strip to add the third border to the quilt top in the same manner, followed by the fourth border using the remainder of the pieced cream strip.

FINISHING

1. Layer the quilt top with batting and backing; baste the layers together.

2. Quilt as desired.

3. Bind the quilt edges with the red 2¼"-wide binding strips.

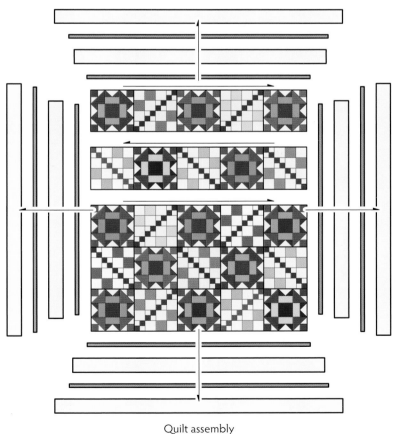

Quilt assembly

Color Option

"Carrie's Fantasy," machine pieced by Ysleta Meek
and machine quilted by Denise Mariano

This quilt is a Rainbow recipe of beautiful batiks and hand-painted fabrics.
Bright and colorful, Ysleta's fabrics truly shine in their own blocks.

Back in Time

Having a huge stash of 1800s reproduction prints from all the major designers, including Mimi Dietrich's line of Smithsonian prints, I was itching to use as many as possible in these old-time Paddle Star blocks. Each block is made one at a time from a Color Family recipe of black, blue, brown, gold, and a light background print.

FINISHED QUILT: 36½" x 36½" • FINISHED BLOCK: 6" x 6" • Make 16 blocks.

SKILL LEVEL:

MATERIALS

Yardage is based on 42"-wide fabric.

10" x 10" square or fat eighth *each* of 16 assorted light background prints

5" x 5" square *each* of 16 assorted black and 16 assorted blue prints

5" x 5" square *each* of 16 assorted brown and 16 assorted gold prints

1⅓ yards of striped print for outer border*

⅓ yard of tan print for inner border

¼ yard of medium-brown print for middle border

⅓ yard of fabric for binding

1⅓ yards of fabric for backing

42" x 42" square of batting

*If your fabric is not a stripe, ⅝ yard will be sufficient.

BLOCK CUTTING

Instructions are for cutting one block. Before you begin cutting, make 16 sets, with one black print, one blue print, one brown print, one gold print, and one light background print in each set. Repeat these instructions for each set to make 16 blocks. Cut the block sets separately in order to keep the prints in each set together.

From *both* the black print and the blue print, cut:

1 square, 3" x 3"; cut in half diagonally to make 2 triangles (4 total)

2 squares, 1½" x 1½" (4 total)

From *both* the brown print and the gold print, cut:

2 squares, 2" x 2"; cut in half diagonally to make 4 triangles (8 total)

2 squares, 1½" x 1½" (4 total)

From the light background print, cut:

2 squares, 3" x 3"; cut in half diagonally to make 4 triangles

4 squares, 2" x 2"; cut in half diagonally to make 8 triangles

4 squares, 1½" x 1½"

CUTTING FOR REMAINING PIECES

From the tan print, cut:
4 strips, 2" x 42"

From the medium-brown print, cut:
4 strips, 1½" x 42"

From the *lengthwise grain* of the striped fabric, cut:
4 strips, 4" x 42"

From the binding fabric, cut:
4 strips, 2¼" x 42"

Machine pieced by Donna Lynn Thomas; machine quilted by Kim Pope

BLOCK ASSEMBLY

Instructions are for making one block at a time. Press all seam allowances in the direction of the arrows.

1. Select one set of block pieces. Arrange two black and two blue 1½" squares into two horizontal rows as shown. Sew the units in each row together. Join the rows to make a four-patch unit for the block center. Release the stitching in the seam allowance of the final seam so that the seam allowances can be pressed in a clockwise direction.

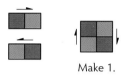

Make 1.

2. Sew a black 3" triangle to a light background 3" triangle along the long bias edges. Repeat to make a total of two half-square-triangle units. Repeat with the blue 3" triangles and the remaining light background 3" triangles. Press. Trim the units to 2½" x 2½".

Make 2.   Make 2.

3. Sew a gold 2" triangle to a light background 2" triangle along the long bias edges. Repeat to make a total of four half-square-triangle units. Press the seam allowances of two units toward the gold triangles and the remaining two units toward the light triangles. Repeat with the brown 2" triangles and the remaining light background 2" triangles. Trim the units to 1½" x 1½".

Make 2. Make 2. Make 2. Make 2.

4. Lay out the half-square-triangle units from step 2 with the brown, gold, and background 1½" squares as shown. Sew the units in each row together. Join the rows. Repeat to make two of each corner unit. Release the stitching in the seam allowance of the final seams so that the seam allowances can be pressed in a counterclockwise direction.

Make 2.   Make 2.

5. Arrange the block center unit, the corner units, and the large half-square-triangle units from step 2 as shown. Sew the units in each row together. Join the rows.

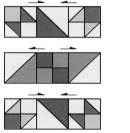 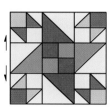

Make 1.

6. Repeat steps 1–5 with the remaining block sets to make a total of 16 blocks.

QUILT-TOP ASSEMBLY

1. Refer to the quilt assembly diagram on page 84 to lay out the blocks in four rows of four blocks each. Rotate the blocks so the black and blue prints alternate positions in each row and from row to row. Sew the blocks in each row together. Join the rows.

2. Measure and trim two tan 2"-wide strips to fit the center length of the quilt top. Sew these strips to the sides of the quilt top. Measure and cut the remaining two tan strips to fit the center width of the quilt top. Sew these strips to the top and bottom of the quilt top to complete the inner border.

3. Repeat step 2 with the medium-brown 1½"-wide strips to add the middle border, followed by the striped 4"-wide strips for the outer border.

FINISHING

1. Layer the quilt top with batting and backing; baste the layers together.

2. Quilt as desired.

3. Bind the quilt edges with the 2¼"-wide binding strips.

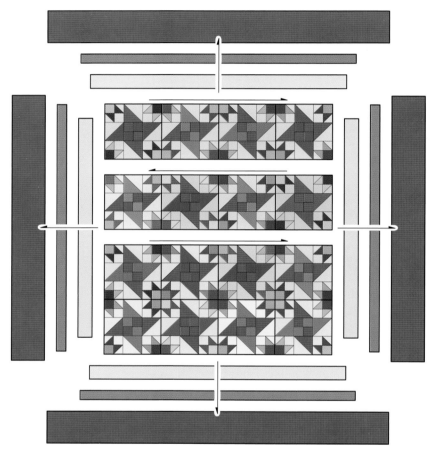

Quilt assembly

Color Option

"Paddle Star," machine pieced and machine quilted by Katharine Brigham

This lovely lap quilt is a Rainbow recipe of bright, sparkly color. You could spend hours looking at all the prints, collected by Kath over a span of many years. She added a pieced border to finish the secondary stars, but other than that, no border is needed for this wonderful quilt.

Turnovers

Even though these blocks are subtle, they feature a Rainbow recipe of colors. With the use of one background print for all the blocks, the quilt becomes a Mixed recipe. For each pair of blocks, choose a dark, medium, and light print in one color family.

FINISHED QUILT: 58¾" x 70" • FINISHED BLOCK: 8" x 8" • Make 28 blocks.

SKILL LEVEL:

MATERIALS

Yardage is based on 42"-wide fabric.

1⅝ yards of cream print for blocks and setting triangles

10" x 10" square *each* of 14 assorted dark prints for blocks

1⅛ yards of dark-taupe print for outer border

6" x 11" piece *each* of 14 assorted medium prints for blocks

7" x 7" square *each* of 14 assorted light prints for blocks

½ yard of rust print for inner border

⅝ yard of fabric for binding

3¾ yards of fabric for backing (horizontal seam)

66" x 77" piece of batting

BLOCK CUTTING

Instructions are for cutting one pair of blocks. Before you begin cutting, make 14 sets, with one dark print, one medium print, and one light print in each set. Repeat these instructions for each set to make 14 pairs of blocks (28 blocks total). Cut the block sets separately in order to keep the prints in each set together. Because each block uses the same background fabric, cutting instructions for those pieces are given under "Cutting for Remaining Pieces."

From the dark print, cut:
4 rectangles, 2" x 3"
4 rectangles, 2" x 4½"

From the medium print, cut:
2 squares, 5" x 5"; cut in half diagonally to make 4 triangles

From the light print, cut:
4 squares, 3" x 3"

CUTTING FOR REMAINING PIECES

From the cream print, cut:
4 strips, 5" x 42"; crosscut into 28 squares, 5" x 5". Cut each square in half diagonally to make 56 triangles.

2 squares, 19" x 19"; cut in half diagonally to make 4 corner setting triangles

2 squares, 13" x 13"; cut into quarters diagonally to make 8 side setting triangles (you'll have 2 left over)

From the soft-red print, cut:
6 strips, 2" x 42"

From the dark-tan print, cut:
6 strips, 5½" x 42"

From the binding fabric, cut:
7 strips, 2¼" x 42"

Machine pieced by Donna Lynn Thomas; machine quilted by Jeanne Zyck

BLOCK ASSEMBLY

Instructions are for making one pair of blocks at a time. Press all seam allowances in the direction of the arrows.

1. Select one set of block pieces. Sew a dark 2" x 3" rectangle and a dark 2" x 4½" rectangle to adjacent sides of a light 3" square as shown. Repeat to make a total of four units.

Make 4.

2. Sew a cream 5" triangle to a medium 5" triangle along the long bias edges. Repeat to make a total of four half-square-triangle units. Trim the units to 4½" x 4½".

Make 4.

3. Arrange two units from step 1 and two units from step 2 into two horizontal rows as shown. Sew the units in each row together. Join the rows. Repeat to make a second block.

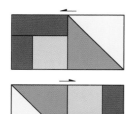 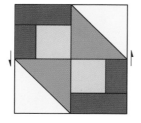

Make 2.

4. Repeat steps 1–3 with the remaining block sets to make a total of 28 blocks.

QUILT-TOP ASSEMBLY

1. Refer to the quilt assembly diagram below to lay out the blocks and the cream side and corner setting triangles in diagonal rows as shown. Sew the blocks and side setting triangles in each row together. Join the rows. Add the corner setting triangles last. Trim the quilt top ¼" from the block corners.

2. Sew the soft-red 2"-wide strips together end to end to make one long strip. From this pieced strip, measure and cut two strips to fit the center length of the quilt top. Sew these strips to the sides of the quilt top. From the remainder of the pieced strip, cut two strips to fit the center width of the quilt top. Sew these strips to the top and bottom of the quilt top to complete the inner border.

3. Repeat step 2 with the dark-tan 5½"-wide strips to add the outer border to the quilt top.

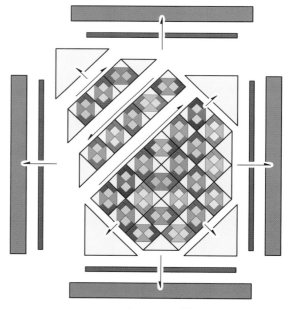

Quilt assembly

FINISHING

1. Layer the quilt top with batting and backing; baste the layers together.

2. Quilt as desired.

3. Bind the quilt edges with the 2¼"-wide binding strips.

Color Option

"Chain Link," machine pieced and hand quilted by Judy Collins

This striking quilt is a Rainbow recipe with all its beautiful bright prints on black. Judy pieced her inner border with squares cut from the block prints, and she did the same for her binding. It's a wonderful way to pull all the block colors to the outside of the quilt. Her beautiful hand-stitched cable quilting with multicolored thread is the perfect finishing touch.

Pineapple Fizz

Refreshing green, yellow, purple, and white prints provide the ingredients for this Color Family—recipe quilt. The blocks are made in sets of two, with the beautiful border print serving as the starting point for choosing all the other colors.

FINISHED QUILT: 60½" x 71¼" • FINISHED BLOCK: 10¾" x 10¾" • Make 20 blocks.

SKILL LEVEL:

MATERIALS

Yardage is based on 42"-wide fabric.

1 fat quarter *each* of 10 assorted green prints for blocks

1 fat quarter *each* of 10 assorted white prints for blocks

1½ yards of multicolored print for fourth border and binding

1 fat eighth *each* of 10 assorted purple prints for blocks

1 fat eighth *each* of 10 assorted medium-yellow prints for blocks

1 fat eighth *each* of 10 assorted light-yellow prints for blocks

⅝ yard of purple print for third border

½ yard of yellow batik for second border

¼ yard of green print for first border

4½ yards of fabric for backing

68" x 78" piece of backing

BLOCK CUTTING

Instructions are for cutting one pair of blocks. Before you begin cutting, make 10 sets, with one assorted green print, one assorted white print, one assorted purple print, one assorted medium-yellow print, and one assorted light-yellow print in each set. Repeat these instructions for each set to make 10 pairs of blocks (20 blocks total). Cut the block sets separately in order to keep the prints in each set together.

From the green print, cut:
5 strips, 2" x 20"; crosscut into 24 rectangles, 2" x 3½"

From the white print, cut:
5 strips, 2" x 20"; crosscut into 48 squares, 2" x 2"

From the purple print, cut:
4 squares, 3¼" x 3¼"; cut in half diagonally to make 8 triangles
2 squares, 3½" x 3½"

From the medium-yellow print, cut:
4 squares, 4¼" x 4¼"; cut in half diagonally to make 8 triangles

From the light-yellow print, cut:
4 squares, 4¼" x 4¼"; cut in half diagonally to make 8 triangles

Continued on page 92.

Machine pieced and machine quilted by Jeanne Zyck

CUTTING FOR REMAINING PIECES

From the green print for first border, cut:
5 strips, 1½" x 42"

From the yellow batik, cut:
6 strips, 2" x 42"

From the purple print for third border, cut:
7 strips, 2½" x 42"

From the multicolored print, cut:
7 strips, 4½" x 42"
7 strips, 2¼" x 42"

BLOCK ASSEMBLY

Instructions are for making one pair of blocks at a time. Press all seam allowances in the direction of the arrows.

1. Select one set of block pieces. Refer to "Folded Corners" on page 7 to draw a diagonal line on the wrong side of each white 2" square. Sew a marked square to one end of a green 2" x 3½" rectangle as shown. Trim ¼" from the stitching line. Repeat on the opposite end to make a flying-geese unit. Repeat to make a total of 24 flying-geese units.

Make 24.

2. Sew three flying-geese units together as shown. Make eight.

Make 8.

3. Sew a purple triangle to the end of each flying-geese row as shown. Press the seam allowances of four rows toward the purple triangle and the other four toward the flying geese.

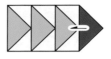 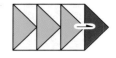

Make 4.   Make 4.

4. Sew a medium-yellow triangle to a light-yellow triangle as shown. Repeat to make a total of eight triangle pairs.

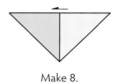

Make 8.

5. Arrange four flying-geese rows, four yellow triangle pairs, and a purple 3½" square into three rows as shown. Sew the units in each row together. Join the rows. Trim the block to 11¼" x 11¼". Repeat to make a second block.

Make 2.

6. Repeat steps 1–5 with the remaining block sets to make a total of 20 blocks.

QUILT-TOP ASSEMBLY

1. Refer to the quilt assembly diagram on page 93 to lay out the blocks in five rows of four blocks each, balancing the prints across the surface of the quilt top. Sew the blocks in each row together. Join the rows.

2. Sew the green-print 1½"-wide strips together end to end to make one long strip. From this pieced strip, measure and cut two strips to fit the center length of the quilt top. Sew these strips to the sides of the quilt top. From the remainder of the pieced strip, measure and cut two strips to fit the center width of the quilt top. Sew these strips to the top and bottom of the quilt top to complete the first border.

3. Repeat step 2 with the yellow-batik 2"-wide strips to add the second border to the quilt top. In the same manner, use the purple 2½"-wide strips to add the third border, followed by the multicolored 4½"-wide strips for the fourth border.

FINISHING

1. Layer the quilt top with batting and backing; baste the layers together.
2. Quilt as desired.
3. Bind the quilt edges with the multicolored 2¼"-wide binding strips.

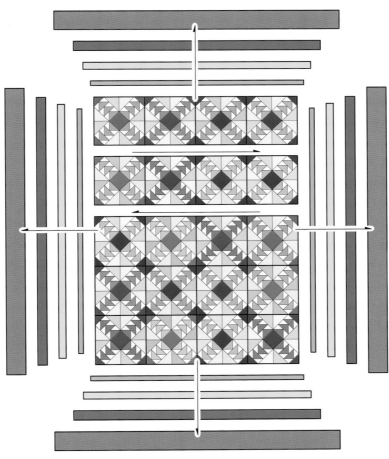

Quilt assembly

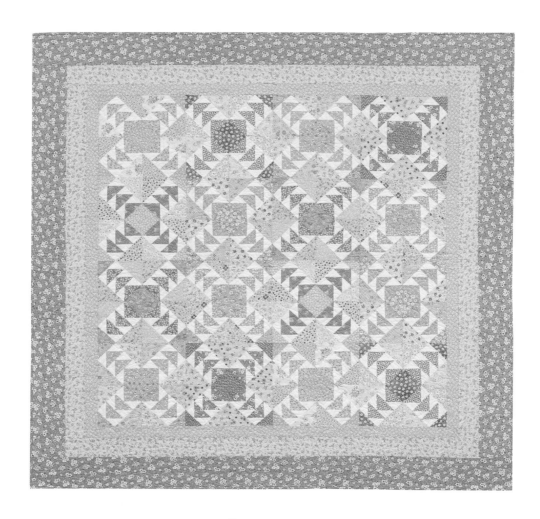

Color Option

"Granny's Sherbet Social," machine pieced by Natalie Hutchinson
and machine quilted by Freda Smith

The colors of the 1930s reproduction fabrics in this lovely and appealing quilt inspired its name. With all the '30s-era prints available now, Natalie couldn't resist using a Rainbow recipe to showcase lots of yummy hues. This quilt would brighten any room it occupies!

Acknowledgments

There is no way in the world I could have made all 26 quilts featured in this book within the time I had. I am blessed to have so many talented quilting friends who are ready and able to make quilts and test patterns. The quilters who finish the quilts are equally amazing. Their work never ceases to take my breath away. A special thanks goes to Shirley Brown, who was my binding angel. What a help you were!

My deep gratitude and thanks go to Carol Kirchhoff, Linda Kittle, Jeanne Poore, Natalie Hutchinson, Kim Pope, Sally Malley, Katharine Brigham, Judy Collins, Charlotte Freeman, Nancy Wakefield, Ann Burgess, Nancy House, Ysleta Meek, Jeanne Zyck, Denise Mariano, Freda Smith, Sandy Gore, Pam Goggans, Theresa Ward, and Alice Scott. The quilts are wonderful!

A special thanks to Nancy Wakefield for reviewing the text with her critical, math-oriented mind. She always provides excellent feedback. I rely on her for honest and clear opinions.

And last, but not least, I give heartfelt thanks to my lovely daughter-in-law Katie, who helps in so many ways with photography, design decisions, readability edits, and providing needed work breaks with visits from Charlotte!

Bonus Project Online

"Mountain High," machine pieced by Donna Lynn Thomas; machine quilted by Denise Mariano.

Visit ShopMartingale.com/extras for complete instructions.

About the Author

Donna has been sewing since the age of four and quilting since 1975. She began teaching in 1981, and since 1988 has been a National Quilting Association certified teacher for basic quiltmaking (NQACT). While an Army wife, she lived in Germany for four years and taught routinely at a German quilt shop and various guilds throughout the country. Long out of the Army, the Thomases have settled in Kansas for good, although Donna's teaching still takes her around the country. The author of many previous titles with Martingale, including *Scrappy Duos* and *Flip Your Way to Fabulous Quilts,* she has also contributed articles on various quilt-related subjects to numerous publications over the years.

Donna's greatest joy is her husband, Terry, and their two sons and daughters-in-law, Joe and Katie and Pete and Nikki. Life just keeps getting better since Joe and Katie added little Miss Charlotte to the family. This absolutely perfect-in-every-way granddaughter (no doting there!) lives minutes away, and loves playing in her grandmother's fabric.

Donna and Terry provide staff assistance to their three cats, Max, Jack, and Skittles, and a kiddy pool and ear scratches to one sunny golden retriever, Brandy. All the quilts in their house are lovingly "pre-furred."

Photography by Katie Lynn Thomas

All grown up now, Jack still loves and pre-furs his quilts. Photography by Katie Lynn Thomas.